EXPLORING
SHIPWRECKS

EXPLORING
SHIPWRECKS

KEITH MORRIS · PETER ROWLANDS

ARTISTS HOUSE

Executive Managers: Kelly Flynn, Susan Egerton-Jones
Designer: Ruth Levy
Editor: Barbara Segal
Production: Peter Phillips, Barbara Hind

Devised and researched by Keith H. Morris
Written by Peter Rowlands

Mitchell Beazley International Ltd
Michelin House
81 Fulham Road
London
SW3 6RB

ISBN 0 86134 107 4

Typeset by Hourds Typographica, Stafford
Reproduction by La Cromolito s.n.c., Milan
Produced by Mandarin Offset
Printed in Malaysia

The joint authors of **Exploring Shipwrecks** would like to
express their personal thanks to the following for their
generous advice and contributions:
Geoff Barker, Michael Mensun Bound, Collins and Chambers Ltd,
Alec Double, Patricia Hipwood, Jack Jackson,
Terry Kruger, Bill Lewis, Amanda Ludlow, Tony Marshall,
Clare Morris, Layla and Lee Morris, Lorraine O'Malley,
Oxford University Shipwreck Trust, Jane Rowlands,
Peter Sieniewicz, Reg Vallintine, Virgin Islands Tourist Board,
Joanna Yellowlees.

CONTENTS

INTRODUCTION

by Reg Vallintine

Few words stimulate the imagination as much as "shipwreck". Down the ages echo the desperate cries of seamen and passengers, trapped in a threatened ship amid wild and breaking seas. Those who have seen the death of a ship are held irresistibly by the sight and the memories never leave them.

For divers today, however, the mention of a wreck brings visions of swimming along companionways inhabited by fish, delving into cabins and over bridges where once humans trod, and above all it brings thoughts of treasure.

For the marine archaeologist, wrecks are "time capsules" in which a moment of time can be preserved in a way that can never happen above the surface. The contents of a seaman's pocket on the *Mary Rose* lie preserved in the silt of the Solent illuminating a lifestyle centuries old; and a tiny fragile oil jug links us directly to the Etruscans and a civilization which existed long before Rome.

For the marine biologist, wrecks are natural laboratories, providing homes for millions of tiny animals and plants which in turn attract thousands of others that graze and prey on them. The sight of the *James Egan Layne* lying on a sand bottom off Plymouth, covered with a carpet of plumose anemones and dead-men's fingers, is never forgotten.

Finally, for the underwater photographer, wrecks provide a dramatic challenge to his techniques and equipment in capturing both the mystery and excitement that he feels, while at the same time recording it all in photographs and on film.

The Eternal Quest

For many centuries, wrecks have provided a profitable source of income to divers searching for cargo or guns, and salvors have sometimes become rich beyond their wildest dreams. Before the birth of Christ, divers in the Levant were employed in the business of bringing up valuables from wrecks. They were paid a percentage of the value which increased with the depth of the wreck.

Since that time, ingenious inventors have produced designs and "machines" to allow man to stay under-

(Right) *Personal effects from The Mary Rose that give an insight into life in Tudor times.*
(Top, far right) *An Etruscan pot saved from one of the oldest shipwrecks in the world.*
(Below, far right) *Marine plants such as large plumose anemones favour wrecks lying in temperate waters.*

water. In 1531 a small portable diving bell, invented by a local man called Lorena, was used to try to raise the Emperor Caligula's pleasure galleys that had lain at the bottom of Lake Nemi in Italy for a thousand years. The bell covered the top half of a man's body and his hands could be used under the rim. By 1658 an improved version of the diving bell was being used down to a depth of 35 metres (110 feet) to recover cannon off Gothenburg, and in early, futile attempts to salvage the Swedish warship *Wasa*, a ship that eventually was raised successfully in 1961. A larger bell that could accommodate several divers was used in 1665 on the famous Tobermory treasure galleon in Scotland recovering several cannons. One of the most successful treasure hunters to use a bell was William Phipps, who, in 1685, brought up treasure worth several millions from a Spanish galleon sunk off Cuba.

The 18th century astronomer, Edmund Halley, recognized and studied the problem of foul air in diving bells; and he came up with a design in which the air could be repurified from barrels sent down from the surface, and by which divers could also work away from the bell for short periods by breathing air through tubes.

The father of diving was John Lethbridge of Newton Abbot in Devon who designed his own apparatus in 1715. He built a tube in which he could lie protected from the water pressure, and look through a small glass window, his hands hanging out of the bottom through two specially insulated holes. He had to be pulled up at intervals so that his assistant could renew the air. Lethbridge could not go deeper than 20 metres (60 feet) because of the water pressure on his arms, but his "machine" worked well and his dream of recovering treasure came true as he travelled the world for the Dutch East India Company.

By 1750 the first, primitive diving helmets were being used. These were usually made of brass with the diver wearing a leather dress. The main problem was water pressure – an atmosphere every 10 metres (30 feet) – which made it difficult to breathe unless the air was fed to the diver at the same pressure.

Two other Englishmen, John and William Braithwaite, designed a special helmet to work on the sunken *Earl of Abergavenny* and they successfully recovered £75,000 in dollar coins from a depth of 20 metres (60 feet). The best helmet, however, was developed by John Deane of Whitstable in Kent. Its use became standard for the next 150 years, and originally it had two large round windows and was fixed to a watertight dress, but Deane improved it further during his 40 years of diving when he worked the wrecks of both the *Mary Rose* and the *Royal George* in the Solent. He was so fascinated by

(Far left) One of the first divers' helmets was this strange bell-shaped arrangement of leather and metal.
(Left) Edmund Halley's bell was supplied with air pumped down from a fire engine. The basic principle behind these diving bells still operates today, even in the commercial diving world.

his discoveries that he made careful sketches of the artifacts recovered, thus making a pioneering contribution to the science of underwater archaeology.

The use of "free" diving apparatus, whereby the diver is independent of air tubes to the surface, dates from the middle of the 19th century. William James in England, and Charles Condert in America both came up with designs which featured compressed air held in a metal reservoir fixed round the diver's waist. A variation on this design came from France and was called the "Aerophore", and in this case a small metal cannister was carried on the diver's back containing air at a pressure of 40 atmospheres. Rouquayrol and Denayrouze, the inventors, also introduced a "demand valve", or "regulator" whereby the pressure of the air could be adjusted to that of the surrounding water by the diver. The equipment proved successful, and Jules Verne equipped Captain Nemo and his crew with an "improved version" in *20,000 Leagues Under the Sea*.

Gradually cylinders were developed that could hold higher pressures of air and by 1900 another Frenchman, Louis Bouton, had a compressed air breathing set with two cylinders holding air at nearly 200 atmospheres pressure.

Much of the development of the present day aqualung or SCUBA (Self-contained underwater breathing apparatus) has taken place in France. Yves Le Prieur evolved an apparatus in which the air cylinders were attached to the diver's back and air fed to a full face mask instead of goggles, and he was a founder of the first diving club in Paris in 1935 using the new equipment. His apparatus was not perfect of course; much of the air was wasted, and the pressure still had to be adjusted manually. In 1939, Georges Commeinhes produced the first fully automatic aqualung with a demand valve mounted between the diver's shoulder blades, and Jacques Cousteau, with engineer Emile Gagnan, produced the final version of it which is used by millions of amateur divers today.

Diving clubs, schools and organizations proliferated in the years after the war and amateur divers became the "eyes under the sea" reporting to scientists, biologists and archaeologists. Inevitably, many of these land-bound experts learnt to dive themselves, and their arrival underwater spawned several important diving techniques as well as major scientific discoveries.

Photography

Back in 1856, a William Thompson had taken the World's first underwater photographs off the

(Far right) *Diving suits developed from diving bells and were advertised in the* Illustrated London News *on November 24th 1855.* (Above) *A contemporary illustration etched on a silver cup shows John Lethbridge, his diving boat, crew and barrel.*

Weymouth coast in Britain. His leaking camera recorded a dim image of sand and seaweed. Then in 1893 the Frenchman, Louis Bouton, used a wet plate camera sealed in a copper housing. It weighed 400lbs underwater and, using a diving helmet, Bouton produced the first underwater flash photographs.

By the 1950s diving biologists, using cameras, had discovered many kinds of nudibranchs or sea slugs unknown when the only means of discovering them had been the net or the line. Underwater photography became not only an important scientific and strategic operation, but a popular pastime, and now fully amphibious and very sophisticated cameras are available, and photographs and films have introduced the underwater world to millions.

History Under the Seas

Underwater archaeology is now a recognized science. The pioneer in this field was George Bass of the University of Pennsylvania, who was the first to excavate ancient wrecks in the Mediterranean to the high standards of land archaeology. The work on the *Mary Rose* achieved worldwide publicity, but that extraordinary underwater excavation was only possible because of the contribution of hundreds of amateur divers who helped the archaeologists with the excavation and survey.

The Dream comes true

The aqualung has given a new lease of life and new hopes of great fortunes to the modern treasure hunter. Mel Fisher, for instance, spent 16 years of patient research and searching in the Florida Keys. Quite recently he discovered the wreck of the Spanish galleon *Atocha*, and he found the cargo too: gold and emeralds worth four hundred million dollars.

The wrecks covered in this book range in time from the Etruscan cargo ship of 600 BC to the *Umbria* and other casualties of World War 2. Locations range from the Mediterranean to the Pacific and from the Great Lakes to Bermuda – seven of the greatest shipwrecks explored by amateur divers. Some, such as the Etruscan wreck, have given us new knowledge of the past. Others, such as the *Umbria* and the *Rhone*, are unique because they are so perfectly preserved and are inhabited by rich sea life. Some have tragic histories, the *Royal Oak* and the Japanese wrecks of Truk Lagoon. Their stories are fascinating enough, but the photographs bring these relics of human endeavour and disaster back to life.

(Far left) This old print shows hard hat divers retrieving the cargo from a recently sunken ship and ignoring the bodies of those who drowned.
(Left) The marine world boasts hundreds of types of nudibranchs. Most of them are brightly coloured.

WRECK SITES

THE
ETRUSCAN WRECK

Ancient shipwrecks provide historians
with vital information about past eras.
In the case of the Etruscan Wreck,
its recovery has revealed more than land
excavations.
The advent of free-swimming scuba diving
has opened up new areas of discovery, but
not all divers have preservation in mind
and rapid recovery is needed to safeguard
the ancient and valuable remains.

The first task of a wreckhunter, through often long and arduous research, is to pinpoint the location of a wreck and then to collect enough evidence to identify it. Hours, days, weeks and often months can be spent ploughing through old manuscripts which give copious, but possibly confusing details of ancient cargoes and of the ships which carried them.

For most divers, the object of their work lies on or under the seabed, undisturbed and undiscovered for centuries. Such locations can have two effects on the wreck. Either the relentless movements of the sea gradually reduces it to a heap of fragmented remains or the marine covering that colonizes it can actually preserve the ship, saving it in a submarine time capsule. In most cases, historic wrecks are first discovered through painstaking research on dry land. Divers only enter the water after the research team has established the most likely site. The more fortunate teams make significant discoveries within the first few dives. For those less fortunate, diving continuously for days and weeks may not produce anything of significance. Such lack of results could lead to the cancellation of a project, an event that could damage the morale and future capability of the team.

Vital clues

Modern technology has provided marine wreck researchers with the means to stay underwater for long periods of time (such periods being limited more by human endurance than equipment). This is achieved by using a breathing apparatus, the aqualung. Since its invention in 1948 it has enabled millions of humans to sample and become, however briefly, part of the underwater world. The interest and activities of so many amateurs has, in many cases, reversed the way discoveries are made. Instead of researching and then diving, they dive first and then, when they surface with man-made artefacts, set about identifying them. However, such advantage in mobility and exploration can, and often does, have negative repercussions.

Such problems have beset a wreck

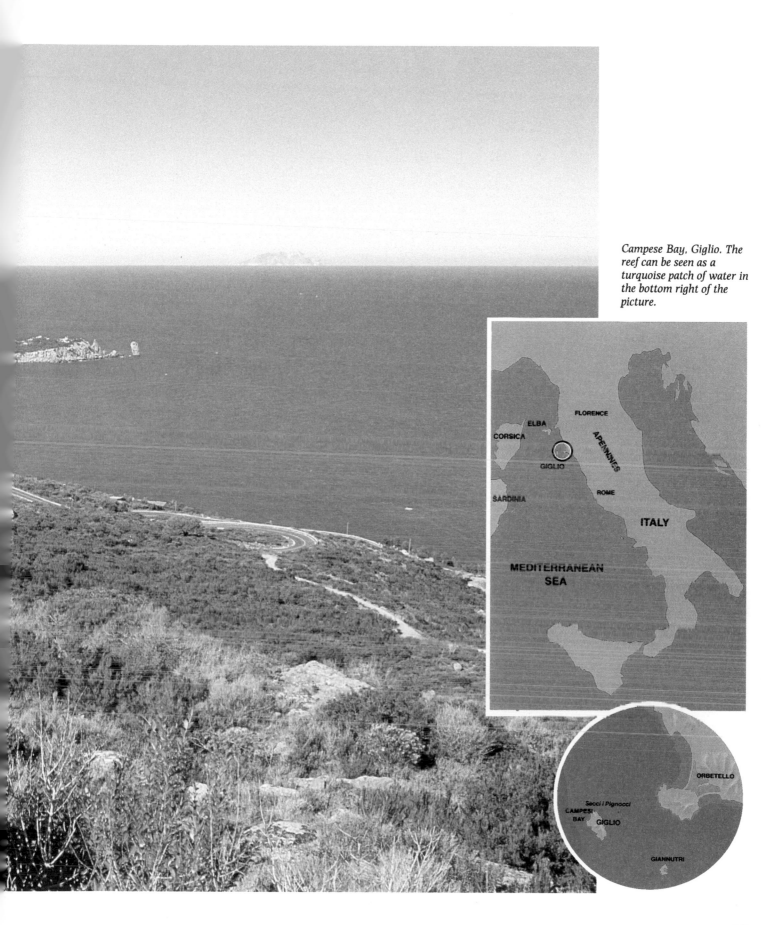

Campese Bay, Giglio. The reef can be seen as a turquoise patch of water in the bottom right of the picture.

FLORENCE

ELBA

CORSICA

APENNINES

GIGLIO

SARDINIA

ROME

ITALY

MEDITERRANEAN
SEA

ORBETELLO

Secci i Pignocci

CAMPESI
BAY   GIGLIO

GIANNUTRI

which was discovered by chance over 25 years ago and is only now recognized as the oldest shipwreck in the world. (It is likely that an even older wreck has since been discovered.) This particular wrecksite has been robbed of some of its most precious and historically vital clues by amateur divers, driven by tales of underwater booty and treasure chests. To an individual diver a single small vase is simply a trophy destined to become a conversation piece on a mantlepiece: to the serious marine researcher it may well provide the vital link in the long chain of clues needed to identify the site.

Today, the site of this ancient wreck, off Giglio island, is a protected reserve. Controlled scientific excavations are taking place around it to unearth new knowledge about an era of which so little is known, the Etruscan era.

(Above) *The extent of the Etruscan Empire.*

(Above) *An Etruscan earing from between 400 and 250 BC.*

(Above) *Callipers found under concretion in 1985.*

Etruscan times

Despite claims that theirs was the earliest culture to write, the Etruscans have left little written evidence to give us an insight into their era. What we now know has been collated from archaeological finds.

The Etruscans lived in the area between the Tiber and Arno in northern Italy. Their land was very fertile and supported rich crops that created their trading surplus. With the sea to the west and the Apennines inland, they were protected and able to flourish. Their efforts brought a great deal of wealth to the area and enabled them to purchase quality goods from the established civilizations of Egypt and Greece. Members of a strong and informed society provided Rome and her empire with the first three generations of kings. The Etruscans could therefore claim to be the founders of the Roman empire and it is certain they were the purveyors of taste and style now associated with the Romans. Evidence uncovered in recent decades shows that the Etruscans enjoyed a high quality of life, with sports and artistic entertainment playing an important part.

The work on Giglio is of such importance that from now on anybody wishing to study the Etruscans would be well advised to study the remains of the excavation. Such work being a tribute to the determination of Mensun Bound and the tireless efforts of a widely differing group of people — academics and divers, professionals and amateurs — who for four years from 1982 to 1986 undertook a major and difficult project which has certainly advanced historical learning.

The importance of such work led to the formation of the Oxford University Maritime Archaeology Research Group, MARE, to continue the study and excavation of wrecks from antiquity.

(Above) A panel of an alabaster cinerary urn showing horseman, musicians and a sacrificial sheep.
(Left) Sarcophagus of seianti Thanunia Tlesnasa.

The discovery

Encouraged by the boom in air travel and financed by a cash-rich society, the diving world in the early 1960s experienced a pioneering explosion, the effects of which were felt both above and below the waterline. Without realising the consequences, if any, of his actions, intent only on making a living from his hobby, Reg Vallintine, a member of the diving fraternity, left his native London to set up one of the first diving schools abroad. He hoped that the warm climate and clear waters of the Mediterranean island of Giglio, just off the west coast of Italy would attract divers to his school as a holiday venue.

Fortunately for wreck researchers, Reg logged his dives meticulously, even though he made repeated dives each day to sites with which he was totally familiar. On 2 August 1961 he logged yet another dive taking a group down into the deeper waters off Campese Bay. His party consisted of photographers and spearfishermen, all looking for their

(Above) *Reg Vallintine at home in London with his log book from his days as a dive guide in Giglio.*

(Left) *The first item raised from the wreck. On the dive during which the wreck was found in 1961, Reg Vallintine had with him another diver called Beryl Boomshooft who slipped this into her pouch. They afterwards decided it was an Etruscan doorknob! Beryl kindly gave this vase to the excavating team, and now it is back with all the other materials in Florence.*

(Near left) Of all the items that Reg Vallintine raised in 1961, and which he hoped would be the core of a new museum collection, only two copper ingots survived. They were refound by the team in an old storage room.
(Left) Draughtsman, Mike Wright, drawing one of the ingots. Rich metal deposits first attracted other nations of the Mediterranean to Etruria.
(Centre) Reg Vallintine and Mensun Bound.
(Below) This Etruscan handle was spotted by Mensun Bound in a private collection in England.

own forms of underwater booty. High on both of their lists would be Grouper — large fish with menacing looks but harmless to man. These fish grow up to 2 metres (6 feet) and were plentiful in the Mediterranean before the advent of snorkelling and then scuba diving spearfishermen.

On this particular dive around a submarine island known as *Secci i Pignocchi*, Reg and his diving party came across a large grouper which seemed to be guarding the entrance to a cave. It was in this area 40 – 50 metres (150 feet) down, that the group found interesting remains and shapes in the sandy seabed.

As word of the wreck spread, the site fast became a client-drawing attraction for Reg. However, despite his need to earn a living, he became increasingly concerned by the amount of individual "souvenir collecting" each time he took divers to the site. He tried to interest the local authorities in starting a small museum but, although the support was there, it was not as widespread as he had hoped. Archaeologists on the island were also indifferent. After a few years Reg left the island and returned to London to continue his career in diving, eventually to become the Chairman of the British Sub Aqua Club.

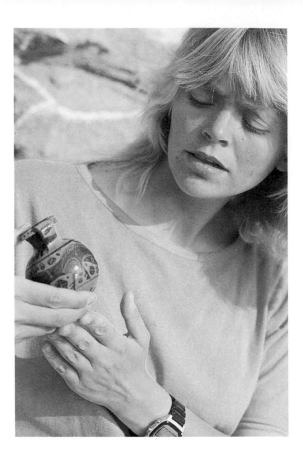

(Right) *Joanna Yellowlees examines a painted Etruscan aryballos. This vase is clearly portrayed in the technical drawing (left).*

Divers no longer visited the site and, for a time, its existence was almost forgotten. New historic shipwrecks, such as the *Mary Rose* in the English Channel were in the headlines. To marine archaeologists this was an ideal opportunity to examine closely aspects of Tudor England, an era when maritime skills were the foundation of the country's widespread power. Investment potential encouraged by Royal patronage, together with the evocative and romantic history of the wreck, created worldwide interest in the *Mary Rose.* It was inevitable that Reg Vallintine would sooner, or later meet an Oxford don, Michael Mensun Bound.

Mensun's consuming interest in marine archaeology drove him to locate and arrange a meeting with Alexander McKee, the first person to find the *Mary Rose.* Mensun wanted to talk about preserving wrecks in general and, in particular, to learn whether the experience gained on the *Mary Rose* might help him in his project to preserve wrecks off the Falklands Islands.

During his first visit to McKee's house, Mensun Bound noticed a piece of rough pottery in the shape of a handle. Alexander had found the artefact while diving with Reg Vallintine in 1963. Mensun was fascinated, and his knowledge of such artefacts led him to believe that this piece dated back to Etruscan times. McKee put Mensun in touch with Reg and the first of many meetings was set up to discuss the Mediterranean site of Giglio and its potential. Mensun was convinced that this wreck held information which would fill in the considerable gaps in our knowledge of the era prior to Roman dominance, over 2,500 years ago.

One of the major problems was that over the years visiting divers had removed many items from the site. Now scattered across the world, it would be necessary to trace these to identify and date the wreck. The existence of these artefacts and their authentication would raise the credibility of fundraising schemes to finance a formal excavation of the site, and would also, convince the Italian authorities.

The research

Undaunted by the enormity of the task, Mensun and his companion Joanna Yellowlees set about locating some of the removed pieces. Their only pieces of evidence were Reg's notes and three old photographs of some of the finds and their new owners before they left the site for good.

Of particular interest was a vase whose existence would establish the wreck's date to within the 20 years between 610 BC and 590 BC. Initially, the whereabouts of this all important vase eluded them, but, after detailed studies of Reg's notes, the owner was tracked to Monte Carlo. Having changed her name twice in the intervening years she was hard to find. When she was located, the study of the vital vase revealed that it was made of yellow clay and painted with a chequered band. Other decorations confirmed a date of close to 600 BC for the wreck. It was the vital evidence they needed to attract the finance necessary for serious underwater exploration to get underway.

(Left) This little amphora from the Greek Island of Samos was found in an apartment off Harley Street in London. (Below) The first item uncovered when the wreck site was refound was the top of a large iron concretion with an Etruscan amphora handle – later stolen – on it.

Rediscovery

To the newly formed team the few remains which they had located on land, together with Reg's photographs, suggested that they had found the oldest shipwreck in the world. However, their own interest and enthusiasm was not shared by any potential financiers. For some time they had difficulty finding outside help. Then, through the co-operation of Professor John Boardman, a classical archaeologist, Mensun and his team secured the backing of Oxford University. It was the support they so badly needed if the project was to have a chance of success.

Eventually, the "Giglio Project" was formed under the wing of the University and the World Ship Trust, an organization set up by Prince Philip some years previously to preserve ships all over the world. Reg was offered the post of Chief Diver which he excitedly accepted as it would lead him back to the area he had enjoyed so many years ago.

For Reg it was to be a nerve-racking time as he dived again and again in the once familiar area without finding the site. It is surprising how the mind plays tricks with the imagination especially

Pottery Wreck

OXFORD UNIVERSITY–
WORLD SHIP TRUST
and SOPRINTENDENZA
ARCHEOLOGICA per la
TOSCANA
Island of GIGLIO

profile of off-shore reef
& site

10M

50m

(Opposite) Divers decompressing under the boats. A waterdredge sits in a sling waiting to be lowered.
(Centre) The excavation team's boats in position over the site.
(Left) Section of the reef showing how the site was excavated.

when you are being relied upon to relocate a site you last visited underwater over 20 years ago. He only had a few days with the team and, in true pioneering fashion, it was not until one of the last days that the site was found again. They were unable to establish good bearings and spent a fraught few days after Reg's departure trying to find the wreck again! Eventually they did, using a metal detector which revealed a large iron concretion on which an Etruscan amphora handle adhered. A short

distance away, Mensun found a small vase used for carrying oil or perfume. Having rediscovered the wreck, sensibly, they now buoyed it.

However, it was to be these buoys that would not only help the archaeological team but would also pinpoint the site for the groups of souvenir hunters who would soon gather in the area.

Diving on the Etruscan wreck

In the warm shallow waters of the Mediterranean, divers do not have to wear restricting wetsuits as the temperatures are so high that a tee-shirt is enough protection from the cold. Go deeper, as the divers on this site had to, and you will experience a strange underwater phenomenon known as a thermocline where the much colder water from the depths meets the sun-warmed shallower water. This meeting of the waters is clearly visible. The colder water is much clearer and has a shimmering quality not dissimilar to mirages seen on hot days on land.

For the diver, the impressive visual appearance of a thermocline is spoilt by the sudden drop in water temperature which it represents. The drop can be as much as 10 degrees so if you are to stay

for any length of time below the thermocline full wetsuits are essential. As if the colder water was not enough to contend with, the greater part of the wrecksite lies in 50 metres (150 feet) of water where the effects of breathing air at such pressure cause temporary narcosis. At this depth, "the narcs", as it is known, can cause a sense of panic and fear which can induce a diver to endanger or even attack his diving companions, or a heady euphoria encouraging him to go deeper and even remove his mouthpiece. However, with acclimatized divers under proper supervision, this should never happen Jacques Cousteau is credited with calling this effect "Raptures of the deep".

A diver's time at such a depth is strictly limited. In order to avoid decompression, you would only be able to spend around seven minutes at such a depth before having to make for the surface. Longer bottom time results in long periods of decompression (hanging midwater in the shallows waiting for the absorbed gases to dissipate from the bloodstream without forming minute circulation-stopping bubbles).

Descending slowly down into the deep blue Mediterranean water through the thermocline and past 20 metres (60 feet), your time underwater becomes as much a recording exercise as a dive. You have to time your dive accurately to make sure you don't stay too long and, at the same time, you have to keep a check on your air supply so that, if you do intend to decompress, you will have enough air to allow this.

In shallow water, it is normal diving practice to make for the surface when your cylinder is down to 50 atmospheres (most tanks start with at least 200 atmospheres when full) but with such a deep dive where decompression is planned, this figure would normally be increased to 60 to 80 atmospheres for sensible safety. It is for this reason that divers working on such a project have to be sufficiently experienced that these considerations and calculations become second nature. They can then go about the main purpose of carrying out the tasks set by the organizers to survey the site.

Still further down, as you dive, the colours and light levels fade; your weight increases as your wetsuit compresses under the water pressure and all sound distorts, muted by the density of the water. You are left with a feeling of intense aloneness, which is both exciting and disturbing. The sensation of diving to depths greater than 30 metres (100 feet) is one of the sport's major, and sometimes fatal, attractions. For some, underwater photography in the bright shallow waters is totally absorbing, but for others the sole purpose of

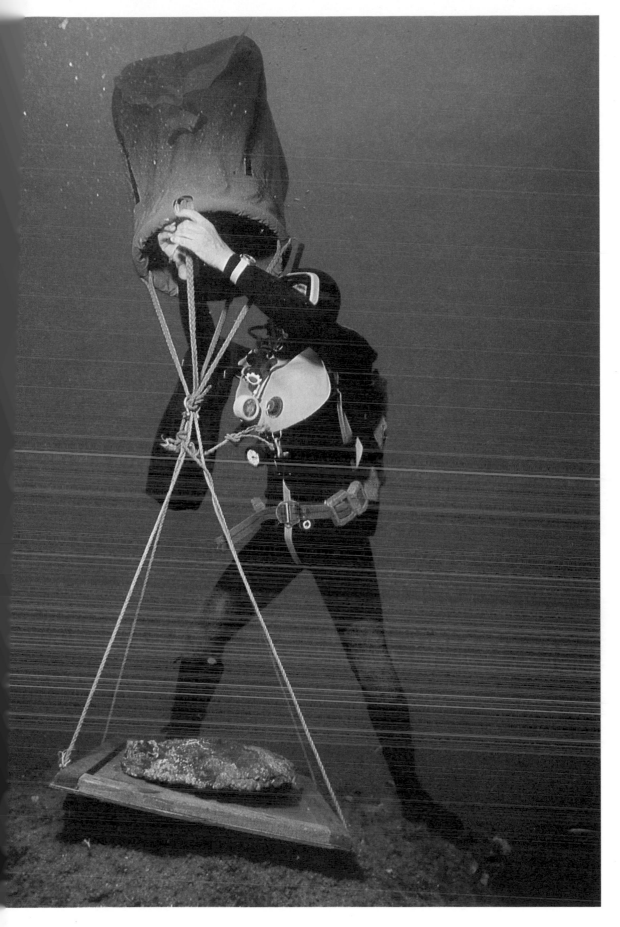

(Far left) *Mensun Bound and Reg Vallintine inspect the ancient remains.*
(Centre) *After working underwater, a diver holds onto the latest find as he decompresses on the reef face.*
(Left) *A lifting bag and tray were used to take heavy objects to the surface.*

diving is to go as deep as possible. The physical limitations of such practices are complicated and personal co-ordination and mental skills become severely reduced. Even for the sport diver, these limitations are relevant but for the marine archaeologist they present a number of problems which restrict the progress that can be made on any one dive.

If the team on the Giglio Project were to make significant progress in such a limited amount of time, they would need many more divers to help them in their work. The academic world of

Oxford, and members of the British Sub Aqua Club, responded with a regular supply of visiting divers on site, attracted not by the money, for they had to pay their own way, but by the thought of diving on and helping to unearth the oldest deep ocean vessel known to man at that time.

Such obvious activity attracted the unwanted bounty hunters and early work on the site, and the project itself, was nearly terminated in early 1983 when, under cover of darkness, unofficial divers took down a portable airlift and sucked up large quantities of

evidence from the site. An airlift is the most economic and efficient way of uncovering large volumes of sand and small objects from an area. Unfortunately, the airlift cannot distinguish between small rocks and delicate Etruscan vases. It will never be known just how much damage was caused both underwater, and to the research in general, as hundreds of vital pieces — including two intact painted Greek vases — disappeared up the airlift's wide suction tube.

In the days following the raid, archaeologists set about sifting through the debris and pieced together fragments to give more evidence of the ship's history. The early problems of underwater piracy were eventually terminated with the help of local police and the use of simple radios so the work could be continued under strict control. Undeterred by the events, the serious diving commenced in the summer of 1983 and by the end of the summer of '84, the team had uncovered many important pieces that were then safely lodged with the Museum of Archaeology in Florence.

In order to record such a site and gain the maximum potential, the area must be referenced so that working divers know exactly where they are in relation to the site as a whole. There are several ways of doing this including the most commonly used permanent grid of iron squares, but as this site covered such a large area, it was decided to depart from traditional surveying methods and divide it into smaller areas dictated by the underwater terrain, each with an identifying name — Victor, Whisky, X-ray, Zulu and so on. These areas were then further subdivided for accurate positioning. On top of the need for accuracy, speed was essential to prevent looters removing precious pieces. In this case, a decision had to be taken to contravene traditional archaeological guidelines: to lift as much material as possible, as quickly as possible, and to make sure that artefacts were preserved in safety for study on the surface.

This practice does not meet with widespread approval within the archaeological world, but it has to be remembered that most archaeologists are used to land sites, generally easier to police. Unless a vessel is kept over an

(Far left) One night, looters broke a big wine-mixing crater. The seabed was later sifted and re-sifted. Fragments – such as the one inserted into the tracing below – were collected in plastic containers, and then pieced together jig-saw fashion in "treatment traps" by the team's conservator. The design slowly emerged of little pot-bellied figures dancing over a row of birds and animals.
(Left) To establish the exact location when pieces were found, a grid system was used for reference. The known size of the grid squares gave scale to the artefacts when they were photographed

underwater site day in, day out, it is difficult to prevent determined looters. Such policing is expensive and not always effective either.

Despite the surface complications, the underwater team began to make several finds which established the identity of the wreck and its original purpose, as well as providing new insight into everyday life over 2,500 years ago. The site, in common with so many ancient wrecks, is difficult to imagine. What the original vessel looked like lying on the seabed with its valuable cargo spilt onto the sand must be kept for the story books, although reconstructions have been done to show her just after sinking. The reality is an unremarkable area of seabed

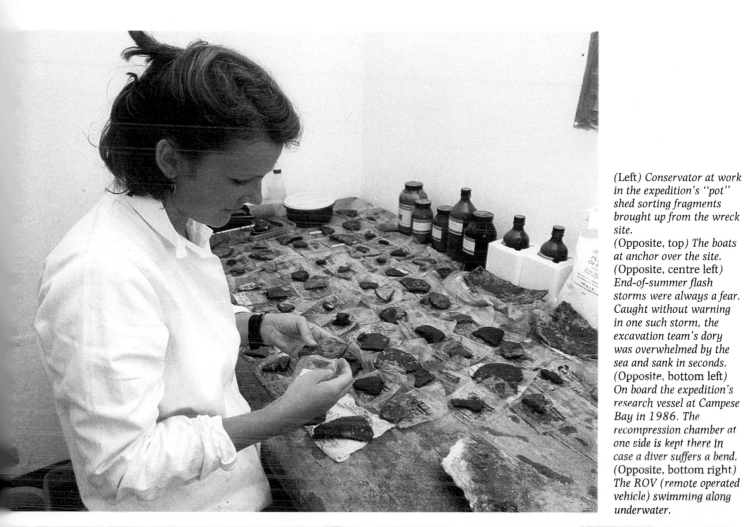

(Left) Conservator at work in the expedition's "pot" shed sorting fragments brought up from the wreck site.
(Opposite, top) The boats at anchor over the site.
(Opposite, centre left) End-of-summer flash storms were always a fear. Caught without warning in one such storm, the excavation team's dory was overwhelmed by the sea and sank in seconds.
(Opposite, bottom left) On board the expedition's research vessel at Campese Bay in 1986. The recompression chamber at one side is kept there in case a diver suffers a bend.
(Opposite, bottom right) The ROV (remote operated vehicle) swimming along underwater.

(Left) Some of the team gather outside the derelict building that was home for five years. The sign reads: "Private property – admission prohibited – Beware Dangerous Building".

(Above) Divers gather for a break beside the excavation truck – the workhorse that made it all possible.

where marine growth combines with large rocks and thick layers of sand dotted with fragments and artefacts.

Speedy excavation by an airlift would mean the possible loss of some pieces as it would inevitably break some items. Careful use of machinery was needed to quicken the removal of sand and light covering debris, but at that depth, a water dredge was more controllable. This simple device passes pressured water from the surface which creates a much gentler and more controllable suction on the seabed. The results of this controlled dredging provided a host of small artefacts such as arrow heads, fishing weights and lump-metal money, all of which combined to give the team a more detailed view of Etruscan life.

The treasures

It is often the case that although some finds are dazzlingly glamorous and large, it is the small pieces which give us a true insight into the everyday lives of the ordinary people of the era under scrutiny. A good example was the discovery of olive pips in some of the Etruscan amphora. They confirmed that the vessel was shipping olives and olive oil. But posed the question whether from or to Italy. Olive trees were not recorded in northern Italy until at least a century after this shipwreck was thought to have occurred, but could these pips indicate a much earlier olive industry in Italy? Olive oil was an important commodity used for lighting, cooking and cosmetics.

In the "Victor" area, large quantities of spilled pitch pine were found. This covered the site where it had flowed out

(Above) An Etruscan amphora full of olive pips; a mound of pips is in the foreground.
A Greek lamp retrieved from the wreck. The charring on its lip indicates that it would have been used on the ship.

Nodules of pitch from one of the amphorae (Far left). After being left in the hot sun for an hour, the modules had melted (left). (Centre, left and below) Two Corinthian aryballoi – one of a goat, the other with a floral motif. (Note the olive pip in the pitch above the goat's shoulder.) The tracings illustrate the "jigsaw" work of the conservators, and show how a Corinthian artist painted his animals and then, after firing, etched in the detail.

of its containers down among the rocks and over many artefacts. Pitch was an important commodity in Etruscan times both as a sealant for buildings and the hulls of ships but also as a flavour-enhancer for the local Retsina-type wine. Careful chipping away of the solidified pitch revealed some more small items, the most interesting of which were several intact and semi-intact *aryballoi* from Corinth. These small round bodied vessels with flat tops and a handle linking the main body to the top were used to carry unguents, perfumes and expensive oils. They are decorated with drawings of wild boars and flowers and came from Corinth, Sparta and Etruria. Even though its solidified mass may contain even more pieces that will prove difficult to extract intact, the pitch has done a fine job in preserving such pieces.

Further finds show that the wreck's cargo also consisted of a consignment flutes and anchors. The flutes or pipes reaffirmed that the Etruscans were particularly fond of wind music. Some of the famous Etruscan tombs are decorated with drawings of musicians playing these pipes. The granite anchor stocks could be identified as originating from a quarry in Italy close to where the ship sank. In common with other excavated ancient shipwrecks, quantities of arrowheads were found, but it has not been successfully established whether these were a trading cargo or a safety supply for the crew to use as a defence against pirates.

(Top) *A single musical pipe, and* (below) *a set of musical pipes retrieved from the wreck.*
(Left) *The two arrowheads in the palm of a hand, give an idea of size. And the drawings illustrate a range of shapes discovered at the wreck.*

10 0   50 cm

(Left) Some years ago
looters were caught raising
stone anchor stocks from
the site. One still survives
in the basement of the local
coastguard building. Here
we see the team with the
stock in the basement.

(Above) A section profile
of the stone anchor stock
illustrated left.

(Below) Another anchor
stock excavated by the
team, was first transported
into shallow water in a
sling under one of the
boats, lowered to the
seabed, and then simply
walked out of the water by
a gang of divers.

The most spectacular find to date was a bronze helmet engraved with drawings of boar and snake heads. This was one of the "finds" taken during the years of Reg's diving school by a German diver. Its existence had been logged by Reg but its whereabouts were difficult to trace since the diver had long since returned home. With their usual tenacity, Mensun Bound and Joanna Yellowlees traced the diver who was now in poor health. He had realised the importance of the helmet and kept it in a bank vault. Anxious that it should remain in his care, he did, however, allow Mensun and Joanna to inspect the helmet and take photographs and drawings of it, worn on the head of a model.

Close inspection revealed that his helmet had been shaped from a single piece of bronze, using skills long since forgotten. Even in Etruscan days it would have been considered a valuable item since it was so well made and exquisitely engraved. Despite persistent pleas, the helmet remains in a German bank vault destined only for its owner's eyes, rather than in the public safety of a museum. It is hoped that one day, this piece will be returned to Italy to form the centre piece of the museum exhibit of the wreck.

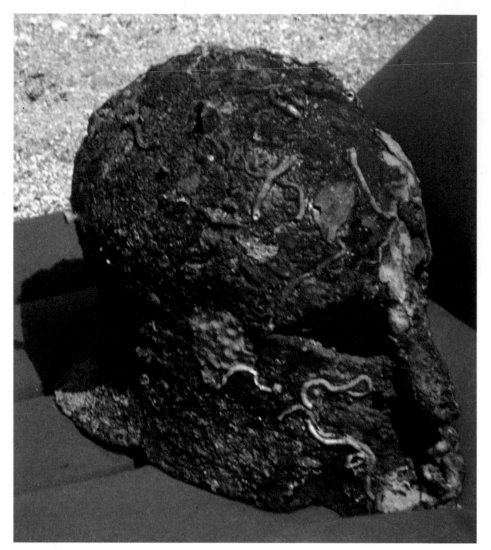

(Right) *This helmet shaped from a single piece of bronze remains the most spectacular find. Its exquisitely engraved detail* (facing and below) *was clearly evident after cleaning.*

During the summer of 1984, the diving team uncovered a large section of the keel of the ship. Initial studies showed this was either made of pine or oak and, though not of particularly complex construction, it gave the first insight into how the Etruscans joined wood to make it waterproof. In 1985, the keel section was raised in the full glare of cameras and press, and brought ashore in a specially constructed box. Detailed study on land showed that the vessel was of "sewn" construction – the main components having being bonded together with cord.

To raise the keel it was first put in a purpose-built box for protection, which is seen (Above) being raised to the surface. (Right) The job of raising large artefacts such as the keel needed several divers and tight planning.

GIGLIO CAMPESE WRECK
DETAIL SECTION A
10 cm
Simon Dobbs 1985

(Above left) *A small fleet
of inflatables were needed
to support the keel and
bring it gently ashore.
(Below left) A detail of the
planking. Cord can be seen
on the tip of the pointer. Of
the ship's hull only a
length of keel and some
strakes survived as
illustrated in the sketches.
These were raised in
1985, and it was a big
media event with TV
cameramen and journalists
descending on Giglio from
all over the world. The
newspaper placards for the
day read – "Etruscan ship
finally recovered from the
sea off Giglio".*

GIGLIO CAMPESE WRECK
THE KEEL – DIAGRAMMATIC RECONSTRUCTION
50 cm
Simon Dobbs 1985

LA NAZIONE
LA NAZIONE GROSSETO

NAVE ETRUSCA
FINALMENTE
RECUPERATA
NEL MARE DEL GIGLIO

Tre generali e centinaia di parà
si sono lanciati a Castiglione

Slittano in curva: feriti 2 vespisti

In Francia Ferrari solo quarta

Giochi della gioventù: 200 ciclisti

THE RHONE

For most ships, their useful lives end when
they sink – often tragically – to the
bottom. But for a few, their location, their
cargo or state of preservation have given
new life. Such a wreck is the *Rhone*, which
sank in a violent hurricane in the British
Virgin Islands. A major attraction for
modern scuba divers, she was also the site
of a Hollywood film.

THE ROYAL MAIL STEAM

Built by the Millwall Iron Works, England. Launched:- February 1865.
Length: 310 feet. Breadth: 40 feet. Displacement: 2738 tons. Accommo

RHONE

...d off Salt Island. October 1867.
...53 first. 30 Second. 30 third.

© Roger Burnett 1981.

Designed & Published by Roger Burnett. P.O. Box 496, East End, British Virgin Islands.

The useful life of a ship ends dramatically when it sinks. It becomes just one more statistic in maritime journals. The memory of the human tragedy fades too. But, underwater, the marine world starts almost instantly to colonize the latest arrival.

There are, however, some instances where the nature of a ship's sinking has brought her more fame than she ever had in her floating career. Such a ship was the Royal Mail Steamship, Rhone, whose two year life ended in one of the worst storms ever experienced in the Caribbean. It was a tragic event for the inhabitants of the British Virgin Islands, and indeed it shocked all the Caribbean island communities. However, before the name of the Rhone was forgotten, the invention of the aqualung stimulated a sudden resurgence of interest in this particular wrecksite.

Divers, seeing the wreck for the first time, enthused about her location and quality as a wreck dive. The word spread throughout the diving world that the Rhone was one of the world's best wrecks. As scuba diving increased in popularity, time has since revealed larger and better wrecks, but the Rhone still has a special reputation which has made her more famous now than ever in her working life.

RMS Rhone

RMS Rhone was commissioned by the Royal Mail Steam Packet Company and launched in February 1865 to serve as a mail-carrying passenger ship in Caribbean waters. Built by the Millwall Iron

41

Works of London, she was much admired for her fine lines, two masts, an abundance of sails as well as her coal-fired steam-driven engine. On board, there were 253 first class, 30 second class and 30 third class cabins together with cargo holds for mail. At 310 feet long and 40 feet wide, she weighed 2,738 registered tons and was capable of 18 knots to speed her from Southampton to South America (with a stopover at St Thomas in the Caribbean US Virgin Islands to take on more coal).

St Thomas was a fast expanding sea port catering for the pioneering packet companies who traded between England and America. In the mid 1800s, however, a scourge of yellow fever swept St Thomas causing visiting ships to transfer to the smaller port of Roadtown, capital of the British Virgin Islands. This smaller harbour had not experienced such rapid expansion but provided sheltered anchorages and easy access to the main shipping channels.

The hurricane

RMS *Rhone* set sail from Southampton on 2 October 1867 and arrived in the British Virgin Islands with a full complement of passengers and loaded with mail. She anchored outside Great Harbour, Peter Island, just across the main channel from Roadtown to offload passengers and take on cargo, fuel and

The usually calm, warm waters of the Caribbean can become a sea of boiling turbulence when hurricane-force winds blow. Such winds are fortunately rare but, when they do occur, the results are often tragic.
(Inset) The nearer to land the more turbulent will be the waters. Here, Black Rock Point looks safe on a calm day but, on the night RMS Rhone sank, it would have been a mountain of foaming spray and raging waves.

new passengers for the return trip to England. She was under the command of Captain Wooley who had anchored her alongside RMS *Conway*, her sister ship, under Captain Hammock. Neither captain expected a hurricane as the season was over. They assumed that a sudden fall in barometric pressure was the signal of a wind arriving from the north. As such a wind would make them dangerously exposed, they decided to head for the shelter of Roadtown Harbour, protected by hills to the north. As a further safety measure, non-swimming passengers were transferred from the *Conway* to be strapped to bunks on the "safer" RMS *Rhone*.

At 11 am, and before they could move, the barometer again fell steeply and a strong wind blew up from the northwest. For an hour, the speed of the wind increased by the minute until it reached hurricane proportions and forced both ships to face the storm with engines running at full power. Any mechanical problems now would have allowed the wind to drive them onto the rocks of Peter Island. After an anxious hour, the wind died down sufficiently for both ships to head for the safety of Roadtown. The *Conway* managed to complete the journey despite losing her funnel and some of her rigging but the *Rhone* snagged her 3,000 lb (1,360 kg) anchor and was forced to abandon it with 300 feet (91 m) of chain. Wooley decided now that the only chance of survival was to head for open water through Salt Island Passage in the hope that they could weather out the renewing hurricane in deeper water away from land.

With the engines steamed up to provide maximum pressure and revolutions, the *Rhone* again battled against the hurricane — which had now altered course completely and was blowing from the southeast. Salt Island Passage was a mass of boiling, foam-covered water, visibility was severely reduced and then, just as open water seemed a possibility, the *Rhone* was hit by an even stronger blast of wind which forced her onto Black Rock Point, the westernmost tip of Salt Island. Her superheated boilers exploded as they were flooded by the cool Caribbean waters. The *Rhone* broke in two and sank instantly in 25 metres (82 feet) of water.

Twenty-three crew members, some of whom were not rescued from the water until the following day, and one passenger, an Italian, survived. It is believed that, of the 173 who died, most were killed by the exploding boilers and the rest were dashed onto the rocks of Salt Island or faced the sharks known to frequent the normally crystal clear and calm waters. The bodies that were washed ashore were buried in shallow graves, covered in the same razor-sharp coral against which the *Rhone*'s iron hull had crumpled on impact.

The ferocity of the hurricane caused havoc to the surrounding islands where over 500 lives were lost and as many as 75 vessels foundered on the rocks or sank at sea. The tragedy had another effect — although not so immediately dramatic — the island lost its reputation as a safe stopover anchorage.

Throughout the Caribbean Islands, the hurricane had brought widespread devastation. Only 18 houses remained on the mainland of Tortola while in Kingston, Jamaica, only four of the original 80 houses still stood.

As the days passed and the hurricane blew itself out, the water calmed down and revealed the *Rhone* with her stern in shallow water just 50 metres (164 feet) from a sandy bay. The *Rhone* remained undisturbed after early bounty hunters, using primitive diving apparatus, managed to salvage some china and crystal together with £60,000 of bullion. The storm, the salvage and the *Rhone* survived in local folklore while the British Virgin Islands returned to comparative tranquility.

"The Deep"

It was not until the invention of sophisticated breathing apparatus, over 100 years later, that the *Rhone* was rediscovered, entombed in waters that are nearly always warm and crystal clear. The abundance of sheltered bays made the Virgin Islands a perfect area for sailors and sports divers. Their proximity to the American mainland has resulted in a highly profitable tourist trade. This has escalated ever since

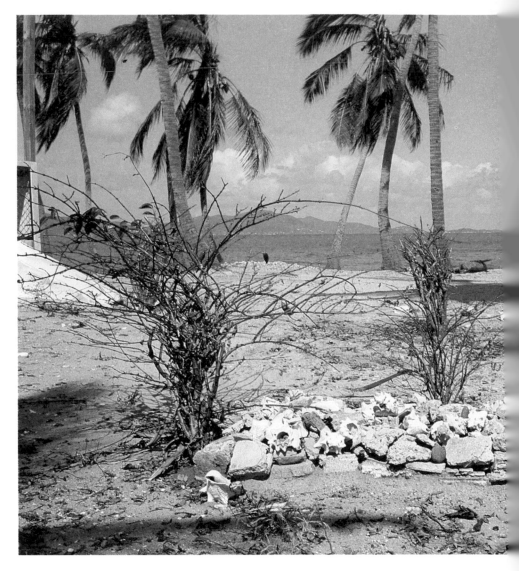

planes could land at the large airport at St Thomas and the smaller one at the northern tip of Tortola.

Divers from all over the world now gather expectantly to sample the beauty of the Caribbean underwater world and, more especially, to dive on the *Rhone*.

Her fame was further enhanced in 1976 when the glittering world of Hollywood film-making descended to use her tranquil setting as a background to the underwater action in *The Deep* — a multi-million dollar motion picture starring Robert Shaw, Jacqueline Bisset and Nick Nolte.

The normally quiet Roadtown was suddenly transformed by the arrival of a large film crew and attendant reporters lured to the site of the most ambitious

underwater film ever made. It was based on Peter Benchley's book *The Deep*, the sequel to his popular first book, *Jaws*. That book had become one of the largest box office successes when it was converted to film by a young and up-and-coming director, Steven Spielberg. *The Deep* was an extremely ambitious project even by Hollywood standards.

Underwater cameramen were consulted for their specialist knowledge and the top job — the shooting of the underwater footage — was eventually given to Al Giddings from the West Coast of America. His first problem was that no camera existed that could film underwater to the scale and quality demanded. So, in the true tradition of

(Top left) *Salt Island still bears the graves of those who perished when the Rhone sank. They are covered in the same razor-sharp corals which ripped open her hull and sent her to the seabed.*

(Above) *Even after countless visiting divers and over a century underwater, artefacts are still being uncovered. The rate at which they are unearthed is increased after violent storms when, even at depth, the powerful water movements on the surface dislodge parts of the wreck to reveal more small items. This delicate clay pipe has survived as well as the more robust glassware.*

(Left) *The Rhone was laiden with a general cargo of wines together with china and cutlery for the crew and passengers, but coral growth has covered most items forever.*

(Far right) The Rhone now lies on her starboard side with her mast firmly on the seabed.
(Right) The saltwater has corroded the Rhone's hull and allows easy access to her insides.
(Below) The explosion of the boilers has left a huge open section into which a diver can swim in complete confidence. The light streams in to illuminate your way.

ingenious film-making, he built three underwater housings for land motion picture cameras. This took just 90 days. The housings not only worked but proved reliable for the entire length of filming.

As an indication of Gidding's drive and flair, he not only produced the housings in shining Ferarri Red but managed to make them with a style and simplicity of operation which reassured even the most cynical Hollywood mogul. Made from cast aluminium to match the contours of the cameras, these housings included external controls which activated all the main functions of the camera. On land they weighed over 30 kg (66lbs) but, under-water, they were neutrally buoyant.

The housings became known as the "Petermars" after the two Peters — Peter Gruber, the producer and Peter

Bisset swimming along the side of the *Rhone* and catching sight of something glittering just inside the wreck. She can't quite reach the tempting item and, as she stretches her arm inside the small opening she is suddenly and forcibly yanked by the arm and smashed against the wreck. The shock makes the audience jump with a mixture of fright and pain as they watch her with her arm still held and then jerked twice more with a terrific force by this mysterious creature inside the wreck. Finally freeing herself, she hurtles to the surface while Nick Nolte tries to restrain her, not knowing what has just occurred. This results in her kicking his valve out of his mouth and further escalating the panic.

What the audience does not know is that the scene is real. The incident happened during another dive and just happened to be filmed by the camera. The director liked the reality of the footage so much that he edited it into the opening action.

The logistics of filming underwater are more complicated than those on land. Communication underwater is virtually impossible except by writing tedious notes on waterproof slates. As a result, detailed briefings were needed on the surface to make sure that when action was signalled the correct movements took place. In addition, time underwater was limited, due to the depth at which they were filming. The crucial scenes were filmed at 25 metres (82 feet) where a diver can stay for only 30 minutes. Staying longer meant time must be spent during the ascents for decompression.

Even so, the filming involved many hours spent decompressing underwater each day. That meant hanging on to a length of weighted rope in mid-water to ensure the correct depth for decompression was kept. The longer you stay down at depth, the longer you have to decompress so the principal cameramen and their assistants were brought fresh air tanks from the surface to keep them underwater as long as possible. Any failure to supply the continuous air tanks would have brought on a massive embolism that would have resulted in slow and painful death. The nearest recompression chamber, where medical

Yates, the director. Both highly acclaimed men in their fields, neither had ever ventured a foot underwater and were more than a little concerned about trying to control the film from the surface. In the end, overcoming their reservations, they learned to dive and then to extend their production skills to the underwater location.

Apprehension about diving was not restricted to those behind the camera. Jacqueline Bisset was known to be afraid of water — even in a swimming pool. Some delicate training was needed, to coax her out of her inbuilt fear. With good and sensitive tuition, she gradually relaxed and felt more and more at home with the valve and equipment necessary to allow her to breathe normally for the first time at 25 metres (82 feet) under the Caribbean Sea.

Three expert underwater camera-men were hired, as was a large crew of assistants to help arrange lighting, lay lighting cables and act as safety cover. Not only was the filming of *The Deep* to be a severe test for the camera equipment but it was also an endurance test for the underwater film crew. They notched up hundreds of underwater hours in the drive to ensure every detail was taken care of.

The film maker had chosen the *Rhone* from a long list of possible wrecks. Relatively undisturbed previously, now, in 1976, she was about to experience an unheralded period of intense activity: 1,465 dives took place within 35 days.

With Jacqueline Bisset much more confident in her diving skills and with Robert Shaw and Nick Nolte already keen divers, the filming could begin. The opening scene sees Jacqueline help might remedy a disaster, was too far away to reach in time.

The actors' time underwater was therefore carefully planned to make most use of the limited time available. They would wait until everything was set before beginning their dives. But, even with this organization and pre-planning, they had to decompress when a particular scene had to be reshot.

After the excitement of filming, the boredom of decompression led to many practical jokes being played on the more experienced divers. Air valves were turned off to see if they would panic, but all the jokers saw was a cool hand reaching back to slowly turn the air on again. Diving safety checks are second nature to such experienced cameramen.

To pass his decompression time more productively, Chuck Nicklin, the third cameraman, perfected the technique of reading a book underwater. The trick was not to let the book dry out for it is then that the paper tears. A carefully handled book lasted long enough underwater for Chuck to finish it.

The job of organizing the diving equipment and safety was given to George Marler who, together with his wife, Luana, had been diving on the *Rhone* for many years. They run the Aquatic Dive Centre on the mainland and have introduced hundreds of divers to the wreck. They have preserved many fascinating artefacts and made several new discoveries including the anchor lost during the hurricane. George's brief from the film makers was to ensure that enough air tanks were filled and ready for use, as well as help with the lighting underwater. He enjoyed 35 lucrative, busy days. Then the Hollywood sideshow left to complete filming in Bermuda. The *Rhone* was left once more as a tourist attraction for visiting divers and an ideal prop for underwater photographers.

Exploring the Rhone

The boat trip across Francis Drake Channel to Black Rock Point, Salt Island, takes just 20 minutes and provides time for a full briefing on the wreck. Your dive boat is anchored carefully over the wreck and the diving platform at the rear lowered to give easy

(Top right) *The prominent bows still remain intact although covered in coral growth. Designed and built to slice through the water at 15 knots this section now lies on a hard rock seabed. Guided dives on the* Rhone *begin here and work back to the stern in shallower water.*
(Right) *The combination of clear water and large open sections make the* Rhone *a safe dive. Inside, the cargo has become "concreted" together into a heap of unrecognizable shapes covered in silt. The more interesting artefacts are to be found on the outside where the water action has discouraged too much growth and so keeps them recognizable.*

access into the warm, clear water. The remains of the *Rhone* cover a large area and lie in depths from 25 metres (82 feet) almost up to the surface. For safe diving it is best to go to the deepest section first and then work your way back into shallow water. Fortunately, this route provides the best opportunity to see the *Rhone* in her entirety. The blue Caribbean waters soon clear even after the rare but sometimes most

violent storms so you catch your first glimpse of the wreck as soon as you hit the water.

The bow section is virtually intact, with the proud bowsprit heeled over and pointing to deeper water. The sleek lines of the hull are still clearly visible lying on her starboard side on a solid rock seabed. The sunlit surface, 25 metres (82 feet) above, provides plenty of general light but a diving torch is a

useful accessory that reveals the true colours of the wreck and the marine growth that has made the structure even more attractive. The water at this depth absorbs most of the colours and leaves only blacks, blues and greys. Your dive light will restore these to vivid reds, greens and purples.

It is the bow section that gives the *Rhone* its special attraction. The traditional bowsprit conjures up images

The most unusual remains
of the Rhone are the
supports for the timber
deck. The deck has rotted
away leaving these iron
columns standing upright.
In the foreground, a small
signalling cannon
protrudes from the
wreckage.

(Above) *A small signalling cannon lies wedged under the wreck. Being iron, it has little commercial value and so has remained in situ since the ship sank.*
(Far right) *The barrel of the signalling cannon has been colonized by marine encrustacean.*
(Right) *The nooks and crannies on any wreck are ideal homes for a variety of marine life. Large Moray eels lurk in the wreckage. They appear ferocious but will only attack and bite if severely provoked.*

of the "tall ships" era when ships were elegant as well as practical and designed for speed and appreciation rather than pure function. This section also gives the diver a definite sense of scale as it is intact save for a few small areas reshaped during the sinking.

The keel faces deeper water and is less interesting than the deck area in between the bowsprit and aft of the foremast. Here, the anchors would have been strapped to the deck with the heavy links of chain leading down to the chain locker below. Rigging would have reached up to the foremast to support auxiliary sails — still considered by the designers of the era necessary to supplement the engines, or to take over in the event of mechanical failure.

Swimming now towards the stern, the first major landmark is the forward mast which now lies as if glued to the seabed. Two-thirds of the way up the mast the crow's nest is clearly visible

and from the very top of the mast you can look back, see the whole of the forward section and appreciate the overall size of the wreck.

The luxury of clear water is often taken for granted by those who have never experienced the claustrophobic darkness of temperate waters after rough weather, but to see whole sections of a wreck in clear water is an experience most divers aim for. Fortunately, the visibility on the *Rhone* rarely disappoints.

To your right as you swim up, the centre section opens up and allows easy access to the inside of the hull. The internal decking has rotted away and fallen to the seabed leaving the site looking like a large warehouse. From the side of the wreck, the davits which once supported lifeboats now reach out in the open water. Behind the davits is an area of columns reminiscent of a classical Greek ruin. They are in fact supporting girders for decking which

has long since rotted away. They rise in serried ranks, superbly decorated by marine growth.

Just below these columns there is a small signalling cannon firmly wedged under large metal plates. These plates are ideal homes for long moray eels that lie with heads protruding slightly and toothy mouths slowly opening and closing filtering water through their gills. The *Rhone* is a catacomb of such lairs, and care should be taken not to be too curious with your hands unless you are absolutely sure that no dangerous animals are at home. Just after the "Greek columns" and 50 metres (164 feet) from the bowsprit, the scene changes dramatically. Here are the boilers that exploded with such force. Fortunately for divers, the explosion opened up an area that allows entry into the main section — a large opening at least 10 metres (33 feet) wide, gradually narrowing as it tapers towards the bows.

Inside, the scene is rather like a scrapheap as areas have either rotted or been blown away. The heaps of mangled metal covered in fine silt are not particularly interesting, but, as you swim slightly further into the *Rhone*, you can begin to pick out light coming from the forward mast area. These shafts of light gradually increase until you come to gaps where you can swim out of the wreck and back towards the bows. The openings are not large but are safe. They were created by doors rotting away from their metal bulkheads. You have to be careful that your air tank does not hit the steelwork and this calls for experienced control over your buoyancy.

Swimming in and out of the *Rhone* is an exhilarating experience. Most wrecks are either so distorted that they are hazardous or are so confined that they are unwelcoming. The *Rhone* feels safe and does not pose problems.

From here, the wreck changes totally. There are no formal structures as you make your way from one piece of wreckage to another. The largest item is one of the boilers and a little to the right, in slightly deeper water, there are the condenser tubes. Further small areas of wreckage lead you into shallower water where the debris changes direction abruptly and leads to your left. The shapes again become more familiar as another boiler appears. The aft mast lies to the left in a similar condition to the foremast but detached from its base. From now on, the waters, being shallower, are much brighter.

The engine lies just aft of the gearbox housing and from here into the shallows your eye is drawn to the massive propshaft that transferred the power of the 600 horsepower engine down to the propeller. The shaft is supported at intervals by steel blocks, easily recognized as they stand above the general level of the seabed. Portholes mark areas that were probably first class cabins but which now lie flattened in 10 metres (33 feet) of water.

(Centre) *Looking out from inside the* Rhone *the blue water contrasts with the black of the wreck. Divers must take care not to snag their cylinders when swimming out through the holes.*

(Top left, inset) *The stern section is in much shallower water with the huge prop still clearly visible.*

(Bottom left, inset) *The main drive shaft runs from the engine, through the gearbox housing and on to the propeller.*

(Left) *The gearbox housing is only just recognizable, as the faster coral growth in the shallower water camouflages the original shape.*

(Bottom left) *One of the blades of the Rhone's massive single propeller was broken as it crashed to the seabed while still turning at full speed.*

Evidence of the lifestyle enjoyed by the passengers now lies encrusted in solid coral. Necks of champagne bottles protrude from the solid marine growth, which will, in time, cover much of the wreckage in shallower water. All over the *Rhone* there is a luxurious covering of colourful marine growth which varies from hard corals to soft filter feeding sponges.

Unfortunately for the careless or unprotected diver, there are large areas of staghorn coral — a hard coral that inflicts a painful sting if touched with an unprotected hand. This coral is covered with minute hairs, just like nettles on land, and contains a painful poison. A thin pair of gloves will reduce the risk but, in such warm waters, short wetsuits are usually worn leaving knees and elbows exposed. Many is the time when a muffled cry signals that a diving companion has experienced a brush with staghorn coral.

Despite such minor obstacles for human visitors, the *Rhone* is an ideal habitat for marine life. The protection of the larger sections accomodates shoals of bluestriped grunts and yellow tailed snappers. In the surrounding areas nutrient-rich sand provides pasture for goatfish, probing avidly under the surface of the sand with their special front feelers.

For those divers who want to attract fish, there is one sure method — food in a plastic bag. You only have to make a move towards your wetsuit pocket to pull out a food bag and you will be

(Far left) *The comical Trumpet fish tries to blend in with the coral for camouflage but is obvious to the diver's eye.*
(Centre) *So many divers have visited the Rhone that the fish are not shy. In fact, they are so friendly that when a bag of food is produced, the feeding diver can virtually disappear in a swarm of pecking fish. They will not go away until they are sure there is no more food.*
(Below) *The various coral growths are both attractive and potentially dangerous. This fire coral inflicts a nasty sting when touched with a bare hand.*

instantly surrounded by a shoal of fish so thick that you will not be able to see open water. The ball of frenzied activity will completely surround you. The fish dart all over you and they will peck at anything. It may be fun for a moment but, after a while, it can become quite claustrophobic. Thrashing your arms to scare them away makes no difference. The only way to escape is to push your way through the ball and gradually the fish will subside as they realize the food has run out.

(Centre) *Delicate tree coral takes years to grow. And it needs clean, sunlit water for fastest growth.*
(Top) *The area surrounding the wreck is a perfect nibbling-ground for fish. Most pick at the softer corals and rummage in the sand for food.*
(Below) *The open structures of the wreck provide safe lairs for all kinds of fish. These Grunt swarm over most of the wreck.*

(Top) These Yellow
Stripes prefer the shelter
between the wreck and the
seabed.
(Above) Funnel-like
sponges like the calmer
waters inside the wreck.
(Centre) The vibrant life
over a coral reef is one of
the thrills of diving – fish,
soft corals and sponges.
(Top right) These
Big-eyes seek the safety of
the wreck.
(Below right) The sandy
seabed can come up with
exciting surprises. This
large Eagle Ray will swim
off slowly if disturbed.

Despite this self-inflicted hazard, the marine life on the *Rhone* is a fascinating revelation of successful colonization. Its conservation is ensured by law, for the site of the *Rhone* is a nature reserve. Several underwater plaques, placed in strategic locations, make sure that it remains undisturbed by the thousands of divers who visit her every year. As long as such laws are observed, the *Rhone* will continue to attract divers from all over the world to the tropical paradise of the British Virgin Islands.

THE GREAT LAKES

The fresh water of the Great Lakes in
North America preserves huge timber
wrecks which represent an era of shipping
that declined as fast as air cargo and road
transport developed.
The action of gale-force winds across a
large expanse of fresh water results in
wave formations that no shipbuilder could
overcome, but it has given the diving
world an exciting legacy.

To most people, inland water is a calm stretch of cold water, usually surrounded by hills and small enough to be able to see the other bank on all but the wildest of days. The Great Lakes, on the border between Canada and the United States of America, cover an area larger than the combined total of England, Wales and Scotland. The longest stretch of uninterrupted water in the area is over 450 km (280 miles) long. With statistics such as these, the Great Lakes move up the importance ladder.

(Above) The Strathern – a fine example of early Great Lakes shipping – was the last of the barques. (Right) Early settlers coped with severe conditions.

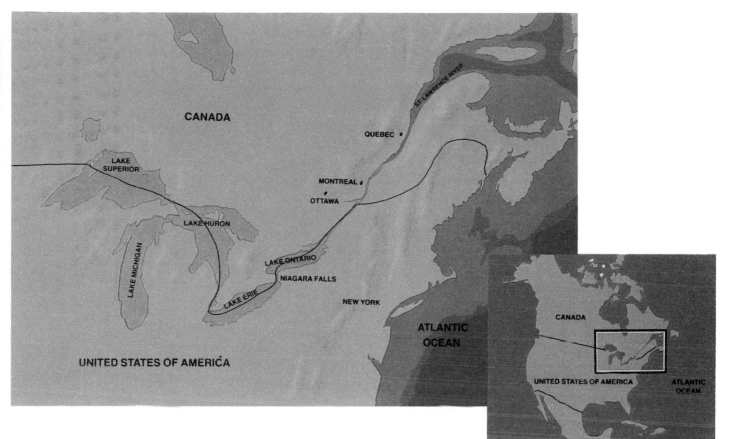

Generally people don't associate shipwrecks with what they instinctively feel are placid expanses of water. Mention freshwater to most divers and you will be greeted with an unexcited response. This almost sterile environment is regarded as one that is only to be tolerated during the winter months when the surrounding seas are too rough to dive but training programmes must continue.

Such attitudes, although understandable and commonplace, are misguided. Not only are freshwater shipwrecks as numerous as those in the open sea, but they are usually better preserved, enabling divers to study their structures and cargoes more easily. The mainstay of this surprising statistic are the five Great Lakes where many such wrecks are to be found. Despite the relatively small area of water and small percentage of shipping involved, these land-locked waterways have contributed to hundreds of shipwrecks. What is staggering is that shipping first came to the Great Lakes just a little over two hundred years ago.

Here in the Great Lakes a combination of physical climate and underwater conditions have given divers an array of interesting sites. These waters are extremely cold and ice cover is a common occurrence. Although physically uncomfortable for divers, this is an advantage: cold, fresh water restricts marine growth and so acts as a preservative. Since wrecks are kept in prime condition, diving on them is much more productive as you can easily recognize sections of the wrecks. Instead of shunning freshwater wrecks, divers should be more enthusiastic about diving on some of the cleanest wrecks in the world.

The Great Lakes

As explorers fought their way all over the globe to make new discoveries and colonize territories, the vastness of our planet became evident. Pleasant and temperate climates were the first to support visitors, and it was not until these had been fully explored, that man ventured into the colder northern climates. Here survival was never guaranteed and the terrain became extremely difficult and hazardous.

The first maritime explorers sailed across the Atlantic Ocean and stumbled on what is now the St Lawrence River. They had no idea at this time that it would lead them to the vast expanses of inland water which would eventually support the gradual colonization and exploration of these then empty and inhospitable lands.

In these days prior to the advent of ice-breaking ships, the St Lawrence was iced over for much of the year as the temperatures dropped from summer highs of 20°C (68°F) down to −10°C (14°F). These may not seem to be too excessive but it should be borne in mind that the average annual temperature is just 5°C (41°F) and the summer highs are short lived. The result is a very damp climate with high rain and snowfall figures. We are, it must be remembered, in an area about 45° above the equator but although this is on the same level as London, the Lakes are in the centre of a huge land mass which does not benefit from the warm waters of the Gulf Stream.

Traders moving up the St Lawrence founded the early settlements of Quebec, Montreal and Ottawa, the capital of Canada. Later, all of these three cities derived their early growth from shipping carrying cargoes from east to west. The traders realised that the huge inland waterways would allow the movement of cargoes over long distances, impossible overland. At first these early traders experienced difficulty in approaching the lakes: the nearer one got to a lake, so it became more and more hazardous. For example, the area close to the Niagara Falls. Here the 50 metre (164 feet) drop had to be bypassed with a man-made canal. Today there are now internationally maintained canals linking all of the five lakes — Ontario, Erie, Huron, Michigan and Superior.

The Shipwrecks

It is the huge size and inhospitable climate of the Great Lakes which have led them to play host to an inordinate number of shipwrecks. No significant naval warfare has ever taken place on their surfaces yet well over 500 ships have sunk in the short time since shipping first appeared in these waterways. Local climate and prevailing winds combined with the effects of the different physical properties of freshwater are responsible for sometimes impossible conditions.

Just as on the open waters of the oceans, the surface water conditions are dictated by the wind. The larger the area of open water, the greater the effect the wind will have. But these facts

*Canada's contrasts:
(Above) Quebec and Laporte Bridges in Quebec span the St Lawrence River.
(Middle) The Desjardins' business complex in 20th century Montreal.
(Bottom) Ships are specially designed to cope with the ice.*

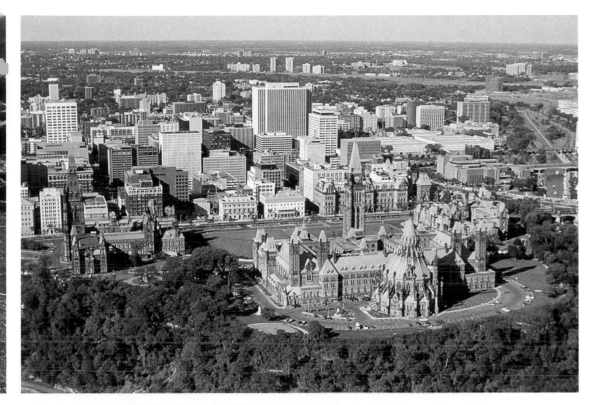

(Left) Montreal, combines modern and old style buildings. Her financial base has stemmed from Great Lakes trading.
(Below) The Canadian mountain ranges present picturesque but inhospitable landscapes. Snow lies most of the year.

and conditions are no different to those experienced in open oceans so why do the Great Lakes pose such a threat? The problem lies in the difference between fresh and saltwater. Saltwater is much denser and so is more supportive and slower to react. As an indication of this increased support, laden ships going from fresh to saltwater will rise around 15 cm (6 inches). Freshwater is whipped up more quickly by the wind and has much smaller distances between wave peaks.

It is this difference that causes Great Lakes shipping so many problems. Whereas a seagoing vessel could plough down into a wave trough and rise up with the peak, fresh water, being less supportive means that the short distances between peaks can lead to a ship going into a trough and never pulling out of it. Wave heights of 13 metres (43 feet) are not uncommon.

In the case of Lake Huron, the winds generate from the northern area of Sault Sainte Marie and pick up speed as they blow down towards the warmer land masses to the south. They travel over the uninterrupted surface of Lake Huron and can raise the water level 3

67

metres (10 feet) higher at one end.

These hazardous conditions are a threat to both large and small ships. One of the largest vessels to sink was a 580-foot ship which went down into a steep trough and just kept going down.

The Great Storm of 1913 is a measure of the power of local conditions. In just one night, the winds blew so severely and whipped up the surface so fiercely that 57 ships, some up to 500 feet long, went down complete with cargoes and this was just on Lake Huron. The cargoes were, in the main, iron ore being shipped from the mineral rich mountainous areas out through the St Lawrence and into the trade routes of the high seas.

Under the Great Lakes

In saltwater, timbers and metals can be quite quickly reduced to powder as marine growth and chemical corrosion etch their surfaces but, in freshwater, there is very little life and the composition does not provide the destructive chemicals so evident in saltwater. Here, structures which have been underwater for nearly two centuries attract very little marine growth. Even in shallow water where there is the maximum of ambient light, the only major growth is a thin layer of weed. The result is clean wrecks, held in a deep-freeze state, awaiting the exploration of divers.

One of the most productive areas for a wreck diver is Georgian Bay to the east of Lake Huron. This is a large extension of the Lake separated by Bruce peninsula at the end of which is Tobermory. A recently published account of the diveable wrecks in the Georgian Bay area listed at least 55 known wrecks. The most prolific area is just off Tobermory where over 20 wrecks lie in close proximity to each other.

The most famous are not only of interest to divers, they are also tourist attractions which can be viewed from the safety of a glass-bottomed boat. The popularity of the wrecks had led to the formation of a 116 square kilometre (45 square mile) protection zone known as the Fathom Five Provincial Park. It extends from Dunks Bay, to the east of Tobermory, to Bears Rump Island in the North East, across to the west to include Cove Island and back to the mainland at Cape Hurd. The aim of the park is to emphasize the historic and natural resources of the marine environment and to promote greater public awareness.

The Sweepstakes

Probably the most exciting wreck in the area is the *Sweepstakes*. Lying in such shallow water that she can be seen from the surface, she plays host to a constant procession of approved observation boats. Built in 1867, the *Sweepstakes* was launched from Wellington Square, Ontario. At 120 feet long, she was an unusual ship by most ocean-going standards in that she had a "drop keel". This design was and still is very common on dinghies and small yachts where storage and access to shallow waters are prime requirements. The use of this drop keel schooner design on larger vessels was that it gave them greater manoeuvrability in shallow water harbours that constant dredging kept operational.

Carrying a cargo of coal, the *Sweepstakes* sank in 1896 probably having suffered damage passing through Cape Hurd Channel in just 8 metres (26 feet) of water. The real facts are still unknown. The *Sweepstakes* is intact but for the stern section. This area was not damaged during the sinking but subsequently has been crushed, separated and moved by ice which covers the area for as much as four months of the year.

For about one month of this period, the ice forms packs rather than flows and is subject to a downward movement. Being up to 2 metres (6 feet) thick, this mass causes more damage each year.

Despite the damage, the *Sweepstakes* is a perfect example of a Great Lakes schooner and her construction can be clearly investigated. Lying just 40 metres (130 feet) from the head of Big Tub, she has continued to deteriorate underwater and is not really a safe wreck to go inside but for those who do, the structure could be weakened by a rush of bubbles causing timbers to fall to the lakebed. There has even been some underwater repairwork undertaken to make the wreck safer for divers.

Most of the surrounding land is privately owned, so access to the *Sweepstakes* is by boat from Tobermory. More energetic divers have to swim from the Government docks in Big Tub, Tobermory, to the wreck site.

(Above) The inland water of the Great Lakes can provide calm, safe sailing. (Left) The open landscape, however, offers little resistance to strong winds that can turn a tranquil scene into a dangerous and rough expanse of water in a very short space of time.

(Far right) *The 120-ft* Sweepstakes *lies in just 8 metres (26 ft) with her prominent anchor winch and gearing still intact.* (Below right) *The solid timbers still remain but they are being gradually eroded by ice which covers the wreck for as much as four months every year.* (Right) *Divers can swim inside the wreck to view her clean timbers, but gradual deterioration has made it risky. To safeguard themselves, divers have started to repair the wreck so that they can explore inside in greater safety.*

Being in such shallow water, the ambient light levels are good but the water can be very cold. A surface temperature of 60°F/15°C can drop by as much as 10° by the time you descend 8 metres (25 feet) so all divers wear full wetsuits, hood, boots and gloves. For the professional and wealthier divers, dry suits make cold water more tolerable.

The sun's rays do penetrate down to the *Sweepstakes* where they provide attractive shafts of light, rather than any significant warmth. The clarity of the water rarely exceeds 10 metres (33 feet) but a lack of planktonic life helps keep the colour cast much bluer than normal. Where there is a heavy deposit of plankton and marine organisms, the

colour cast of the water is usually heavy green. This becomes darker and darker, the deeper you dive.

Reflecting the difficulties she was in prior to her sinking, the *Sweepstakes* is in a poor state, with decking rotted away and crucial structural supports in danger of folding. Although this makes her internal areas more accessible there is constant risk of shifting timber. The light levels are high: the sun's rays stream down through the holes in the decking and there is plenty of room for a diver to swim without feeling claustrophobic.

The ribs of the ship and her general timber construction details are clearly visible both internally and externally. At the bows, the solid keelstrip still

stands proudly vertical, but the attached smaller timbers show signs of marine wear and tear. Also, at the bows of the *Sweepstakes* is the large anchor winch with its two capstans and central gearing. The railings running the length of the vessel are still intact, but towards the stern they break up, as does the ship itself, crushed by successive years of grinding ice.

Open hatches allow the safety-conscious diver to view the inner areas from a distance and perhaps they are sensible as well as safe for the coal cargo leaves wetsuits in a dirty state.

The last ten years have seen a rapid deterioration of this wreck. Eventually, the *Sweepstakes* will crumble as a result of ice weathering.

The wreck of the City of Grand Rapids

To add to the attraction of the area around Tobermory, there are another 20 wrecks in shallow water. One of these, the *City of Grand Rapids* is situated close to the *Sweepstakes*. Although this 122-foot long steamer lies in just 3 metres (10 feet) it is not as accessible as the *Sweepstakes*. Over the years, silt has partly buried her and when she sank she filled with debris.

Built in 1879, the *City of Grand Rapids* was a wooden steamer designed to carry passengers and cargo. On 29 October 1907, she was lying at anchor in Little Tub when a small fire broke out on board. Fanned by the wind, the flames soon went out of control and the crew fled. The tug, *Clucas,* was hired to tow her out into open water but the heat from the flames was so intense that they had to cut loose and watch the *City of Grand Rapids* drift towards the head of the Big Tub. Here she went aground, continuing to burn until the flames were extinguished when they reached the waterline.

Underwater, the structure which was not burned is now covered in silt. The larger engine section with its huge boiler remains intact. The rudder and propeller were lifted in 1968 and are on display in the local Peninsula & St Edmunds Township Museum.

(Far left) Close to the Sweepstakes *lies the* City of Grand Rapids. *Sunk by fire, her remaining structure is covered in silt but the engine and boiler section is still evident. (Above) The once solid timbers have slowly rotted leaving the retaining bolts exposed. Being in shallow water, the* City of Grand Rapids *can be visited by divers and snorkellers. (Left) Just below the surface, the remains of the wreck have suffered from wave action and silt.*

(Top right) Being in deeper water, the Arabia has remained impressively intact. Even the chains from bowsprit to the deck are still in place.

(Above) Her huge hull lies upright in deep water and provides an interesting dive for experienced divers. But, the combination of cold water and depth has proved fatal to some novices.

(Below right) One of the main prizes on any wreck is the anchor, and the Arabia's is prominent on her deck.

(Right) As well as her anchor, the Arabia still displays her main wheel which has served as a "prop" for many underwater photographers.

The Arabia

Just outside Tobermory's harbour, the wreck of the *Arabia* lies just off Echo Island in 33 metres (107 feet). Carrying a cargo of 20,000 bushels of corn, she sprang a leak during a fierce gale on Lake Huron on the night of 4 October 1884. Early next morning the Captain ordered the exhausted crew to abandon ship. From the lifeboats, they watched as the 131-foot *Arabia* sank beneath the waves.

It was to be her cargo of corn which would give divers an indication of her whereabouts. Searching the area, they asked local fishermen about the best fishing areas since fish are known to favour wrecks. The fishermen not only told them of a good area but volunteered that the fish they caught there nearly always had black corn in their stomachs. A more concentrated search revealed the wreck of the *Arabia*.

Lying in deep water, the *Arabia* is reached by passing through two thermoclines. Depending on the time of year, these thermoclines move up and down but the temperatures at depth do not vary much. It is a consistent 2°C (36°F) when you dive below 25 metres (82 feet). This mind and body-numbing temperature could account for the high number of diving fatalities which have occurred here over the years.

Once again, the only advantage for divers of such low temperatures is the preservation of the wreck in good condition. The intact bows still have chains lined out from the main winches and the bowsprit provides a powerful photographic subject when silhouetted against the light which just reaches down from the surface. A classic anchor lies strapped to the deck and probably most interesting of all, the ship's wheel still stands in position. Here divers pose in traditional and now somewhat hackneyed way as if they were the captain going down with his ship.

The *Arabia*'s location will keep her intact for some time to come and her reputation will grow as an excellent deeper dive. The most worrying aspect is that she seems to attract novice divers who frequently underestimate the adverse conditions which must be endured to view this example of Great Lakes shipping in its heyday.

Mapledawn

At the head of Georgian Bay in 10 metres (33 feet) lies one of the Great Lakes most popular wreck dives.

The *Mapledawn* was launched in 1890, a 350 foot steel-hulled steamer displacing 3100 tons. In 1924 she went aground during a snowstorm and despite her size, became a total loss. Sections of the wreck were removed in salvage work undertaken during World War 2.

Nevertheless, she is still an excellent dive just 100 metres (328 feet) from the shore. At low tides her bows break the surface, so locating her is easy and she provides safe holds to tie a boat up to. As you drop into the cool waters you cannot fail to be impressed by the twin boilers which are at least 5 metres (16 feet) in diameter. The lack of growth and shallow water will afford you a clear view of this large wreck with its huge decking and plates, some of which are buckled from the salvaging. About 15 metres (49 feet) away from the stern, lies the propeller, the tips of its huge blades broken off by the impact of going aground on the west side of Christian Island.

As with most large wrecks, the engine and boilers remain solid, providing perfect compositions for underwater photographers to capture on film.

(Left) *Despite being partly salvaged during World War 2, the* Mapledawn *is still an impressive sight and, being in shallow water, the light levels are good and the water is slightly warmer.*

(Top, far left) *The huge twin boilers are the most prominent part of the* Mapledawn. *They are each over 5 metres (16 feet) in diameter and will remain intact long after the rest of the ship has flattened.*

(Top left) *Twisted metal surrounds the intact boilers with their huge retaining bolts.*

(Above) *The steel hull has been ripped apart during salvage but still retains its shape. Holes in line show where solid rivets would have held one plate against another.*

(Top right) *Slightly deeper than the boilers is the large single propeller which suffered major damage when the ship sunk. The tips of the blades are broken off.*

(Centre) *The* Michigan *lies in such shallow water that snorkellers can dive down to view the winch gearing.*
(Top, far left) *The rudder of the* Thomas Cranage *lies on a rocky lake bottom.*
(Below, far left). *The propeller of the* Seattle *is about 2 metres (8 feet) across.*
(Below) *The anchor of the* Marquette *lies on sand with her impressive hull upright behind.*
(Left) *The anchor chain of the* W.L. Wetmore *will remain in its untidy heap for centuries.*

The future of the Great Lakes wrecks as sites for divers, tourists and marine life is being preserved by the formation of marine reserve parks. This will help to provide a selection of dives for the keen wreck diver. As waterborne lake transport declined in the 20th Century, the possibility of new wrecks has decreased. However, since there are so many existing wrecks, it is difficult to imagine divers ever running out of wreckdives on the Great Lakes.

THE UMBRIA

If one wreck has stimulated an interest in
the underwater more than any other, it
must be the *Umbria*. First explored by
Hans Hass and made famous in his books
about diving in the Red Sea, the *Umbria*
forms one of the finest centres for scientific
study – she supports a wide and colourful
variety of marine life – and photographic
enjoyment.

Originally owned by The Hamburg South American Lines (a major line in Hamburg where she was built by Reihersts), the *Umbria* started her service in 1912 as the *Bahia Blanca*. In 1935 her name was changed to the *Umbria* (sometimes spelt *Umbrea*) after she had been sold to the Italian Company Lloyd Triestino Di Navigazione and was registered in Genoa.

At 491 feet long and 59 feet wide, the *Umbria* was a twin screw cargo ship that, for most of her life, was connected with South America as a destination and as a country of ownership. Her maritime life was the uneventful transportation of cargoes from one port to another and, like thousands of other vessels, she fulfilled a basic function, earning a living for her owners.

The events of 1940 brought an abrupt halt to her humdrum life. On 12 June 1940, the news that Italy had entered World War 2 and allied herself to Germany reverberated all over the world, particularly in places where Italians lived and traded. The *Umbria*, at this time, was in the British-controlled Port Sudan, half way down the west coast of the Red Sea, and she was carrying a cargo of cement and munitions en route to Rangoon via Eritrea.

She lay at anchor off Wingate Reef. British reaction to Italy's alliance was swift: all Italian assets in Port Sudan were taken over. They included the *Umbria*, just about to set sail. The British Authorities trustingly, or

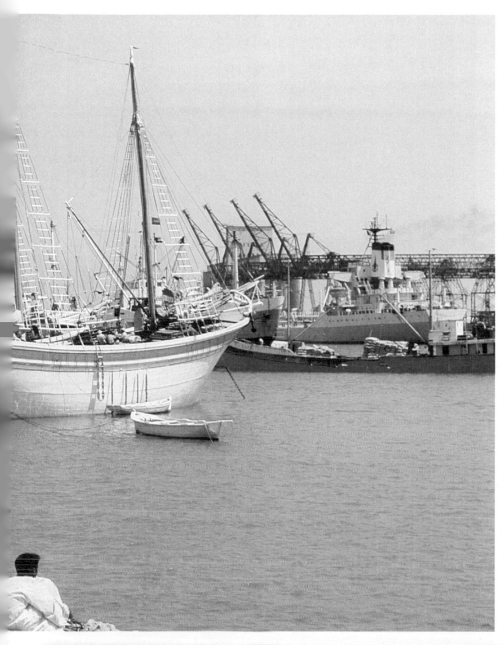

stupidly, assumed that her crew would obey orders from their new owners, and certainly the *Umbria* needed a sizeable crew to keep her operational. But the Italian crew, once the gravity of the situation had sunk in, decided otherwise.

They opened the ship's seacocks and very effectively, denied the British the double prize of the *Umbria* and her cargo. The *Umbria* was slow to sink, so, in order to prevent any attempt to save her, the Italians declared that timed fuses had been placed in the holds that contained large quantities of munitions. The British had no choice but to let her sink.

Location

The *Umbria* sank in an area of busy shipping movements in and out of Port Sudan – the most important harbour on the whole length of the Sudanese Red Sea coastline. It was not the sort of place where any obstacle was likely to be ignored, but strangely enough it was her cargo of munitions which saved her from salvage. Any plan to remove the new obstacle was blocked for fear that the salvors could trigger the increasingly unstable cargo. Had she been blown up, the detonation would have resulted in the generation of a huge tidal wave. The concave shape of Wingate Reef would have reflected this back on to Port Sudan, and the conse-

(Above) *Ships of all nationalities have used Port Sudan to take on cargo and supplies.*
(Left) *The glowing sunsets reflected in the waters of the Red Sea inspired early settlers to give it its name.*

quences of such a wave on such a strategic port could have meant the difference between victory and defeat.

Early underwater explorers

So, despite the inconvenience of her new location to the harbour and shipping authorities, the *Umbria* remained where she sank on one of the most prolific coral reef areas in the world. After the War, these reefs provided a superb environment for the famous adventurers, Jacques Cousteau and Hans Hass to carry out some of the first underwater scientific research on the rates of growth of corals and marine life. Previous expeditions had taken them to possible locations all over the world but, finally, it was the reefs around Port Sudan on which these pioneers chose to spend so many productive years diving and carrying out their underwater scientific experiments.

Cousteau built the very first under-water habitat. Inside it scientists could stay underwater for days, both observing marine life and conducting research into diving medicine. Later on, other research groups came from England to continue Cousteau's work. They set up research platforms on the tops of the reefs as well that provided non-stop access by divers to the shallow coral waters where the diversity and quantity of marine creatures was so attractive.

For Hans Hass, however, it was the *Umbria* herself which first captured his imagination. He was the first civilian to dive on her after the War and his book *Under The Red Sea*, first published in 1952, found a large and enthusiastic public. In his book, he describes how he managed to dive on the *Umbria* initially without official permission in late 1949. The wreck was protected to safeguard the volatile cargo but, of course, her location was hardly a secret, for she lies with her starboard davits breaking the surface in just over 20 metres (60 feet) of water at the stern.

(Centre) *One of the first underwater habitats was set up by Jacques Cousteau to establish rates of coral growth as well as man's ability to survive long periods underwater. The structure has attracted a luxurious growth of Table corals.*

(Inset top, left) *The Cousteau habitat is shallow enough for snorkellers to dive down and inspect in more detail.*

(Inset below, left) *Close to Cousteau's habitat is the "garage" where divers stored their underwater vehicles.*

When Hass first visited the *Umbria*, there was no such thing as an aqualung breathing apparatus: he had to dive using an oxygen rebreather set which limited his time and depth to 10 metres (30 feet). Below this depth the partial pressure of the normally life-sustaining gas would become dangerously toxic. Such a limitation did not deter him, as most that is fascinating about *Umbria* is in such shallow water that any experienced snorkeller can easily explore this huge artificial reef. In fact this was how Hass first investigated the *Umbria* as he did not wish to waste his precious oxygen supply until he was sure that a particular dive was worth using the breathing set.

Even from a snorkeller's restricted viewpoint, Hass appreciated immediately the wealth of the *Umbria* as a natural science resource. The tropical sun and the clear shallow waters provide a nutrient-rich environment and, over a surprisingly few number of years, a brand new structure for the developing marine life to colonize. By 1949, the *Umbria* was transformed into a garden of multi-coloured corals through and around which almost solid

(Top) *The combination of sunlit waters, a sheltered location and low pollution provides ideal conditions for fast and profuse coral growth. The deeper you go, the less the light and the slower the coral growth.*
(Bottom, far left) *The shelter of the Umbria's large structure is ideal for swirling shoals of Glass fish. They part as a diver approaches and then quickly reform.*
(Bottom left) *Portholes, once watertight windows, are now just playthings for the fish to swim through. The brass porthole surrounds remain intact mainly because visiting divers could not carry them back on an aeroplane!*

shoals of a huge variety of fish sauntered in search of food and shelter. "Teeming" is an often over used word, but it was accurately used here by Hass to describe the marine life he saw.

The rapidly developing life on the *Umbria* has been left unchecked and, indeed, since she sank it has been positively encouraged. There is a total ban on fishing around the wreck and on unapproved visitors of any sort. Such a ban

Corals are quick to form on any new structure, given the right conditions. Soft coral grows rapidly while hard coral takes longer.

has provided today's visiting diver with a unique opportunity to experience nature's progress when she is set free of man's restrictions.

For Hass, it must have been an incredible experience as he floated, hovering over the *Umbria*, the very first diver to see her and her newly acquired marine life. Of his second dive he says, "I now considered her almost in the light of a personal possession that I had won in a competition".

Umbria's topside career may not have been particularly eventful but she now provides a foundation of such fecundity for all forms of marine life that her name will never be forgotten. A surface view of a wreck is often particularly restricted as we are now so used to the freedom of the modern aqualung. But on wrecks such as the *Umbria*, surface observations are quite spectacular. In the shallow water around the starboard davits, the main gangway stretches along the side of the ship and provides a much-photographed, perspective-enhancing location as the uniform steelwork recedes into the sunlit background.

Slightly deeper in 15 metres (49 feet) but still visible from the surface on a good day is one of the massive propellers. The port screw is buried but the starboard one stands high above the seabed and, supported on its A frame, provides a rare "prop" for underwater photographers.

(Far left) The main companionway on the Umbria *lies in shallow, sunlit water and recedes into the distance. As she is on her side, the deck is on the left.*
(Left) One of the two huge propellers protrudes from the upturned keel. This bronze prize is prime salvage, but is well protected.

Umbria's modern visitors

Hass's explorations took him away from the *Umbria* soon afterwards, but by then he had brought it to the attention of the diving world and fired the imagination of non-divers with his tales of adventure. And this was at a time when the world's media were looking for anything to brighten up those drab post war years.

Despite the difficult and often uncertain journey to Port Sudan, the *Umbria* continues to attract divers who come from countries all over the world. Several groups have tried to organize diving centres but at the *Umbria*, they experience great problems not only coping with the authorities but also in attracting suitable local labour. Some of them managed to cater for visiting divers with remarkable ingenuity but the difficulties have forced most of them to give up.

One English company has consistently offered an almost uninterrupted facility, although recently this too has ceased to offer diving trips. It was very basic and was based on the lighthouse reef of Sanganeb where a small concrete platform, built to support the lighthouse, also served as a base for the divers. The continued survival of the company was due mostly to the efforts of an English couple, Jack and Babs Jackson, whose experiences organizing trips into the desert mountains of Sudan have given them invaluable local knowledge. The Jacksons have survived many years on the platform, and, despite working with the most primitive facilities, they have been able to sustain and support hundreds of divers who have been attracted over the years from all parts of the world to live right next to some of the most exciting diving in the underwater world.

The Jacksons greet divers in Port Sudan and then take them on the two-hour boat trip to Sanganeb — a route which passes the *Umbria*. The boat is always laden, not only with the newly arrived divers but also with exotic fruit and food from the Port Sudan markets. (The Sanganeb lighthouse boasts no luxuries other than mattresses and a couple of Calor gas cookers.) During the trip, the Jacksons relate the history of the *Umbria* to the new arrivals as they

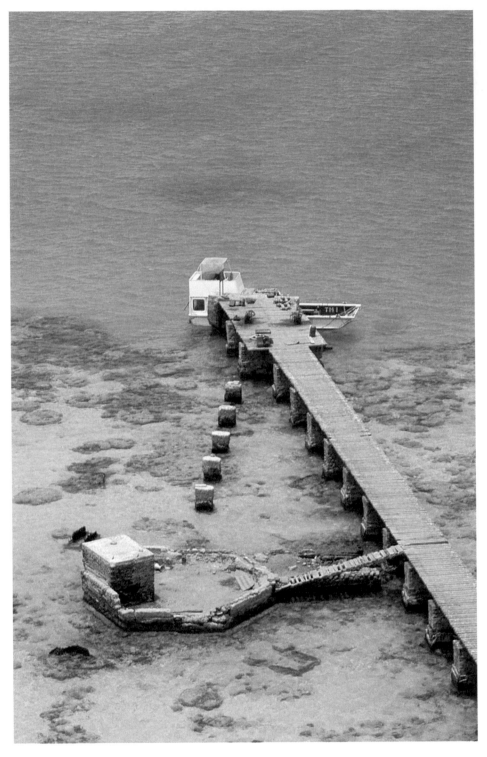

motor past, and there is the promise that they will return to dive on her as soon as they are settled on their new "home".

Diving holiday companies, not surprisingly, establish themselves where diving is good and also attracts enough visitors to be reasonably profitable. In Sudan, it was quite different. It was almost impossible to run a consistent holiday service. It was only the quality of the reef diving, plus the existence of

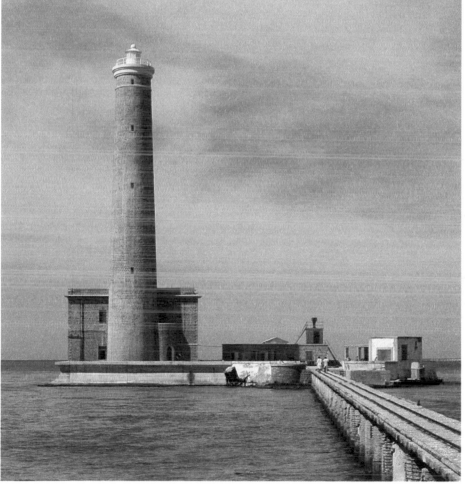

(Far left) *Visiting boats to the Sanganeb Lighthouse have to tie up to the end of the jetty and carry goods along to the main platform on the reef.*

(Top) *A makeshift habitat built by Cambridge University was the home for marine biologists who dived at regular intervals to record and measure the rate of coral growth in the area.*

(Left) *The towering lighthouse operates automatically and warns approaching ships of the treacherous reef.*

the *Umbria* that ensured that enough fee paying customers would brave the red tape and the very basic hospitality.

Hass returns

When Hans Hass decided to revisit the *Umbria*, exactly 30 years after he had first set eyes on her beautifully colonized structure, it was the Jacksons who played host to him. A great deal of change had occurred in those years, diving equipment and training techniques had been researched and developed so that almost anyone could, with proper training, dive in safety and comfort.

Kitted up with the latest air cylinders and demand valves, Jack Jackson and Hans Hass dived the site that brought back so many exciting memories for Hans, and that was now almost a second home for Jack. Armed with photographs taken by Hans during his first visit, they discovered that very little had changed on the wreck itself, apart from the collapse of the funnel, one mast and a lifeboat davit. However, the marine life had multiplied and spread dramatically to cover every area of the wreck.

(Above) *The stern section of the* Umbria *is a mass of curves and corals.*
(Above right) *The open structure of the wreck is a delight to swim around in the bright, clear waters.*

(Right) *Inside the* Umbria *there is no coral growth, just a layer of very fine silt, and divers must be careful not to stir this up.*

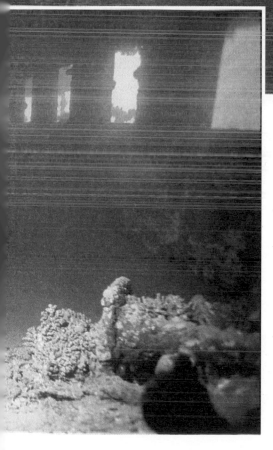

The wreck

When presented with such a wealth of fascinating marine life it is often easy to overlook the structure upon which such life depends. But the structure of the *Umbria* is still too impressive to be ignored, and has not become so over-grown that it is unrecognizable. Indeed the *Umbria* remains virtually intact and her colourful colonizers are an added decoration to an already graceful shape. Particularly impressive is the stern section where her sweeping curves and mainly intact railings slant up towards the sunlit surface. The area is open yet intact and allows divers unlimited and safe access from here to the main holds. The solid steel deck supports are still as strong as ever but the hatches have either rotted away or fell off when she sank. The holds lie at about 45° and are easily accessible to inquisitive visitors.

Inside each hold, the original cargoes are sometimes hard to identify, hidden by a coral coating. In some of the holds, small items have spilled out and lie in jumbled heaps. Elsewhere, large cans of food have been gradually opened by saltwater corrosion, their contents long since eaten by the fish. The holds containing ammunition are to be avoided as some types of explosives become more volatile when steeped in salt water while other types are diffused in time by the marine penetration. There is no knowing which type is which, so total caution is the safest rule.

One of the great attractions of the *Umbria* is that she is so explorable inside. Being in shallow water the light levels are high, so the Umbria's internal areas are pleasantly lit once your eyes become adjusted. Most of the hatches are large enough to swim through and open enough not to worry about them suddenly closing with you inside. As with all wrecks, the internal structures are coated with a deposit of fine silt and care is needed when finning to keep disturbance to a minimum, especially if you wish to photograph the inside.

If the perspective-enhancing gangway is the external attraction on the *Umbria*, it is the porthole-lined internal gangways which are the most photogenic. The contrast between the bright beams of light streaming in through the port holes and the dark green internal decking provides irresistibly powerful compositions. The strongly directional lighting flickers on the decking and gives the internal areas a fireside-dappled, green glow.

Perhaps a few visiting divers have collected the odd small souvenir to remind them of their visits on the *Umbria*, but the larger exhibits still remain. The *Umbria* is a whole ship untouched by salvage or treasure hunters, with uniquely rich marine life and an ideal position.

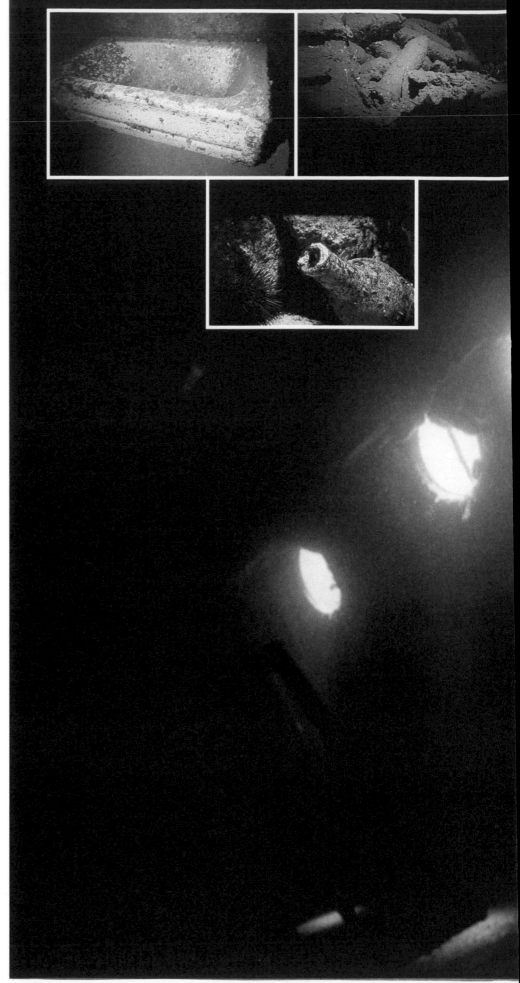

(Centre) *The portholes allow light to stream inside onto the internal bulkheads adding colour, motion and mood.*
(Above, left) *This is one bath which has definitely overflowed forever.*
(Above, right) *The* Umbria's *cargo included munitions en route to Rangoon. These now lie covered in silt.*
(Above, centre) *Wine bottles have long since lost their corks and become a foundation for marine growth.*

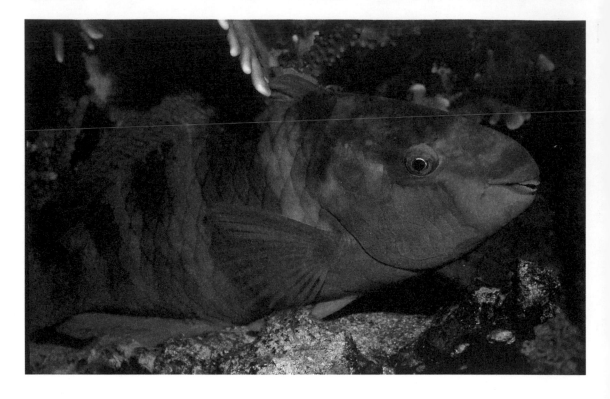

Umbria's marine life

One of the major fascinations for divers on the *Umbria* today is the magnificent range of underwater sights; hard and soft corals have taken advantage of all suitable structures from bulkheads to ammunition boxes and from thin rigging to solid decking. The new habitat created by this gradual colonization has attracted a great variety of marine animals quick to take advantage of all it has to offer. Strange nooks and crannies on the old wreck have taken on new functions as ideal lairs for safety conscious creatures such as Moray eels. Crustacea of all kinds are also attracted by the new sources of food which generate rapidly. The *Umbria* has now found a new and much more interesting role with her natural cargo than ever she achieved in her working life on the surface.

The fast-growing soft corals were the first to take hold of the ship as their needs were ideally suited by these calm clear Red Sea waters. The *Umbria* provided a multitude of places to settle upon and the waters were rich with floating planktonic life — two essential ingredients for profuse marine growth. At the same time that the soft corals were discovering their new homes, bottom-dwelling crabs and lobsters discovered the *Umbria*'s array of wholely

unnatural but particularly suitable lairs. Whether made of iron, timber, hessian or rubber, the critical factor appeared to be position, safety and food supply.

The growth of the coral led to the cautious arrival of many varieties of reef fish. They found the changing face of the *Umbria* an easy source of food and, of course, shelter. Coral-eating Parrot fish, with their powerful beaks were spoilt for choice as they sauntered around the wreck, picking here and pecking there at the corals. The brightly coloured, oblong and rather stubby bodies of the Parrot fish have enough power to thrust themselves at the hard coral to break off food. Their reward from such thrusts is a mixture of algal food and coral. The coral passes through the Parrot fish's digestive system and is eventually deposited as fine sand. This group of fish, of which there are 13 species in the Red Sea, are the largest producers of sand. They feed during the day, flitting from one coral head to another, never resting but, at night, they secrete a veil-like mucus around themselves, settle down into the corals and rest.

Fish attract other fish: bottom-dwelling Lizardfish, for instance, are fun to watch. They lie motionless with their drooping mouths slightly open waiting for small fish to stray into their area. As

soon as one appears, the Lizardfish pounces with lightning speed, grabs the prey, gradually swallowing it whole.

There is no more striking example of effective camouflage than the Scorpionfish, whose family are masters of two kinds of disguise. Not only can they change their colour to blend with the background but they can also change their texture to make seeing them extremely difficult. Like the Lizardfish, they lie on the bottom, motionless and invisible. They, too, rely on prey approaching them — whereupon they spring up to inject their victim with paralysing poison contained in their dorsal, pelvic and anal spines.

Within the same family are two of the underwater world's most famous fish, the Lionfish and Stonefish. The former are noted for their remarkable beauty and grace as they glide over the reefs like underwater galleons. The latter are grotesque but perfectly camouflaged carriers of the most deadly venom known underwater. They are difficult to see even when they are pointed out to you, for they take on the same warty mud-covered texture of their surroundings. Their stout dorsal fins contain the poison which is so painful when injected that it can, and frequently does, cause a fatal heart attack. Because they are perfectly disguised, we divers fortunately never know how

(Far left) *Pastel-coloured Parrot fish eat the corals, digest the nutrients and deposit the rest as sand.*
(Left) *This master of disguise is the Stonefish. It can change colour to blend perfectly with its background and the poisonous spines on its back can be lethal to those unfortunate enough to step on them.*
(Below, left) *The exotic Lionfish hovers majestically in mid-water. Despite its attractive appearance, the long top spines contain poison.*
(Below, right) *During the day, these Parrot fish dart around the corals, biting off chunks with their powerful beaks. At night they use holes in the same coral to sleep in.*

close a brush we may have had with these fish, and, though antidotes are available in some countries, the poison acts so fast that there is rarely time to bring a patient ashore, let alone to a local hospital.

On the lighter side, brilliantly coloured Squirrelfish seek the shelter of overhangs, of which there are many on the *Umbria*. When left alone, they hang motionless beneath their artifical umbrellas, but at the first hint of threat raise their dorsal fins in a fine aggressive display to repel invaders. Their large dark eyes and drooping mouths give them a sorrowful look which even the dorsal display cannot hide. If they are seriously challenged, they soon slip into the corals where the labyrinth of internal holes gives safety.

In the more open areas of the *Umbria*, such as the main holds, big Groupers are to be found. Prized for their size and taste, these fish were the main target for early spearfishers who snorkelled down as far as they could and for as long as possible to kill these docile and highly territorial creatures. The *Umbria* now is not so easily accessible to the casual fisherman and so has provided comparative safety for some really large Groupers in its dark holds.

Harmless to man, the Grouper family feeds mainly on small fish supplemented occasionally by crustacea. Their large mouths have a powerful suction force which effectively vacuums the prey into their mouths. But it is the smaller varieties of Groupers — the Anthias, whose presence most typifies all that is exciting about the Red Sea reefs. The Anthias constantly dart around in shallower water, hugging the coral reef for protection. An approaching diver will see them flitting to the safety of the corals but, within seconds, they are out again in more open water to feed on the plentiful zoo-plankton. Ironically, these little fish are frequently the food of their much larger relations.

The first fish the visiting diver will notice, are those that have learned to associate them with food. The advent of relatively cheap air travel and, even if difficult to organize, the diving package trips have ensured that the *Umbria* has become — for the fish — a renowned feeding station. The most commonly

(Centre) *The majestic Emperor Angel fish glides around the wreck.*

(Inset, above) *Cardinal fish prefer the safety of overhanging table coral.*

(Below, left) *A food carrying diver becomes the centre of attention for Sergeant Major fish. They are voracious eaters and will peck at anything.*

(Below, right) *The graceful Queen Angel fish swims around on its own They are usually very timid, but they have become so used to divers on the* Umbria *that they will take food from their hands.*

used food is left-over bread. At the first appearance of a diver the area is instantly filled with countless small fish of all kinds. They seem to appear from nowhere.

Armed with a plastic bag full of bread, the diver is literally mobbed by silver and black Sergeant Major fish, Snappers of all colours from black and white to pastel yellows and pinks. Small Wrasse and Damselfish also join the riot as a swirling ball of fishlife envelops the new arrivals. Anyone, it seems, remotely likely to bring food with them, is fair game for a peck from the fish. First-time divers often find their ears being nipped by hungry fish. Small they may be, but when you are underwater and you feel your ear being attacked, the instant reaction is to believe it is some big fish intent on inflicting much more damage on their next lunge. A rapid turn, of course, reassures that there is nothing more than the same swirling ball of small fish.

For a more sedate introduction to the *Umbria*, it is better to descend into slightly deeper water where the feeding fishlife becomes more individual and cautious. The larger and prettier Angelfish used to hold back until a diver had receded to a safe distance. But now, with the graciousness their names suggest — Queen, Emperor, Arabian and Royal — they have gradually become more used to human intruders and, after years of patient encouragement, will glide in towards bread held in the fingers and fearlessly suck it in their delicate mouths. The old hands take such activities for granted but, when a shy fish feeds like this for the first time, there is an excitement which is only perhaps equalled by the discovery of a new species.

To find larger fish, one has to look

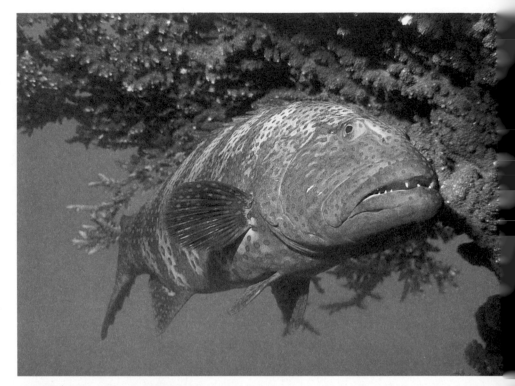

(Above) *A large grouper hovers under an overhang. Despite their looks, they are very shy.*
(Top right) *Clown fish and anemonies live together in a symbiotic relationship.*
(Right) *Shoals of Barracuda swim relentlessly around the Umbria. They have a menacing appearance but have not been known to attack divers here.*
(Below, centre) *The smallest nooks and crannies are put to use by Blennies.*
(Far right) *Anthias abound in the wreck.*

more into the waters just away from the wreck where small shoals of Barracuda circle the area. The Barracuda shoals here are smaller than those off Sanganeb Reef where it is not uncommon to be totally surrounded by a wall of hundreds of barracuda, each measuring anything up to 1 metre (3 feet) in length. To see them in such numbers can give rise to panic as they have a menacing presence. But there is no record of any attacks on divers unless they have been seriously provoked. With a solid wall of these barracudas around you, you cannot help but feel only minor reassurance from these statistics.

The *Umbria* is an attraction of sorts for larger Sharks too, but these scavengers of the sea tend to find the ocean going, rubbish-depositing cargo vessels anchored off Port Sudan far more to their taste. These cargo boats dump the remains of their galleys into the sea, and this waste attracts sharks of all kinds in search of easy food. It is this plentiful supply within the environs of Port Sudan itself that helps keep the *Umbria* a safe place to dive.

The reefs around the Umbria are frequented by numerous varieties of shark. Their reputation makes any diver uneasy.

Jacques Cousteau and his team, on an expedition to observe sharks in the 1960s, set up underwater observatory cages 30 metres (98 feet) down from their underwater habitat on the Sanganeb reef. In those early days of underwater discovery, little was known about the habits of sharks. Tales of shipwrecked sailors being eaten alive as they waited to be rescued were accepted as fact. Cousteau and his team, no doubt very cautious at the prospect of finding out about sharks' habits the hard way, soon found that they were essentially shy creatures — quite capable of attacking man, of course, but only when he provoked the situation with blood-soaked fodder. And it is an interesting fact that nearly all of the most successful photographs of sharks have been taken after they have been attracted in this way.

(Top, right) The much-abused Puffer fish inflates himself to appear more fearsome. Once inflated, however, they can barely move.
(Centre, right) The rigid Box fish cannot swim very fast but is shy of photographers.
(Below, right) The delicate Butterfly fish usually swim in pairs around the wreck pausing here and there to peck at a piece of coral (far right) before moving on.

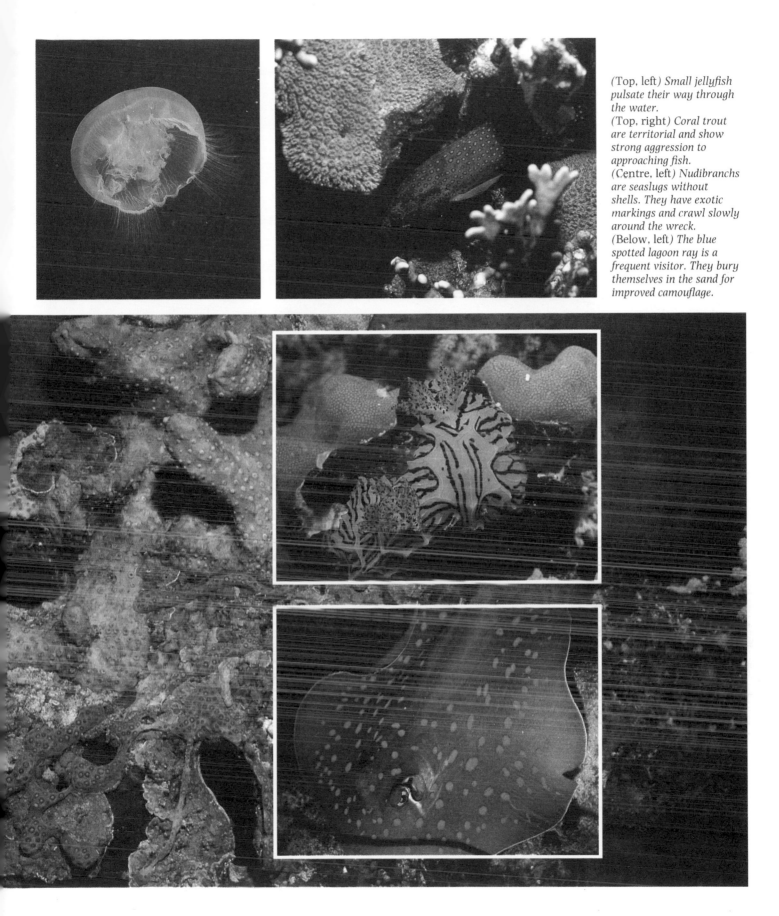

(Top, left) *Small jellyfish pulsate their way through the water.*
(Top, right) *Coral trout are territorial and show strong aggression to approaching fish.*
(Centre, left) *Nudibranchs are seaslugs without shells. They have exotic markings and crawl slowly around the wreck.*
(Below, left) *The blue spotted lagoon ray is a frequent visitor. They bury themselves in the sand for improved camouflage.*

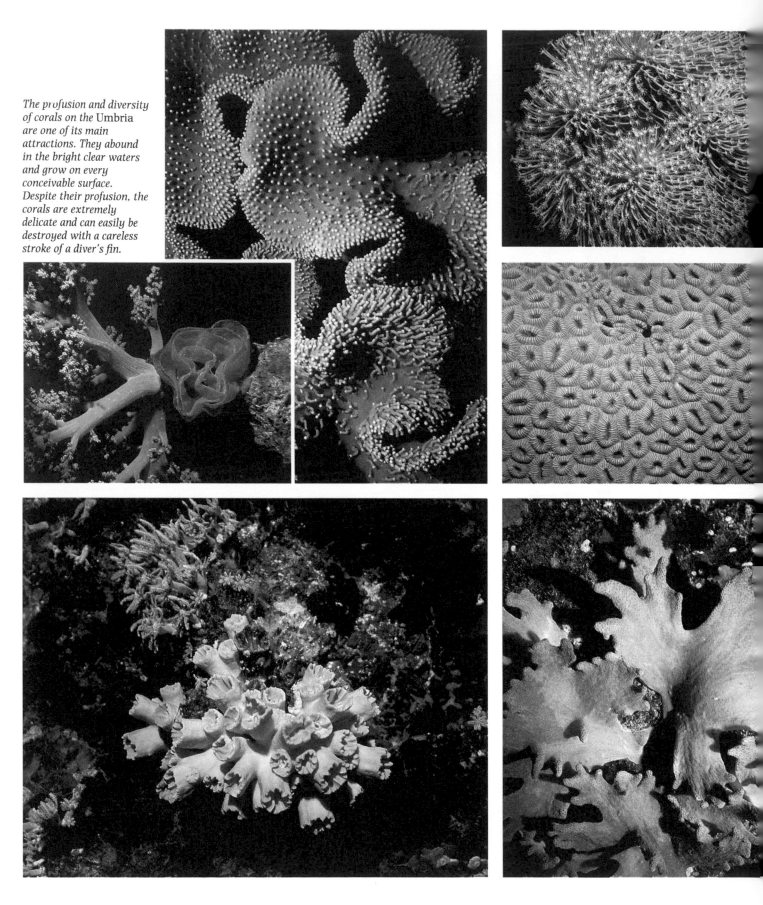

The profusion and diversity of corals on the Umbria are one of its main attractions. They abound in the bright clear waters and grow on every conceivable surface. Despite their profusion, the corals are extremely delicate and can easily be destroyed with a careless stroke of a diver's fin.

Visiting divers cannot fail to respond to the marine life that has colonized the Umbria. The rate of growth of the corals directly correlates with the increase in fish species and other plant and animal life.

THE ROYAL OAK

In 1939, a German U-Boat penetrated
Britain's main anchorage and sank one of
her capital ships. Over 800 men lost their
lives as the great battleship sank. H.M.S.
Royal Oak is a war grave now and may be
dived on only with permission from the
British Royal Navy.

On the night of Friday, 13 October 1939, the British battleship *H.M.S. Royal Oak* was lying at anchor in the north east corner of Scapa Flow — a naturally protected area of water in the Orkney Islands just north of Scotland. What was to become World War 2 had just broken out and, for the second time this century, Britain was at war with Germany. Scapa Flow had once again been chosen as the main anchorage for the British Navy to provide the same facilities available during World War 1.

In one of the worst naval tragedies of World War 2, the light of dawn would reveal this huge 600 foot battleship lying upturned in 30 metres (98 feet) of icy cold water, her seemingly impenetrable hull, already fitted with extra protection side bulges, having been blown apart by the torpedoes from a German U-Boat in one of the most daring and successful raids in the history of maritime Germany. Over 800 British seamen were to lose their lives as the *Royal Oak* sank within minutes and

plummeted to the seabed just a few hundred yards from the safety of the cliffs at Gaitnip.

Miraculously, nearly 400 of her crew survived. Those who were not taken down with the ship were thrown into the icy oil-covered water in total darkness to make heroic attempts to reach the shore or to be plucked from almost certain death by the crew of the tiny tender *Daisy 2*. This boat, no more than 100 feet long and only 15 feet wide, managed to rescue 386 men. They

(Below left) *The 600-foot Royal Oak with her four pairs of 15-inch guns was built in World War 1 but, by 1939, was not as fast as the modern ships.*
(Below) *She displaced 29,000 tons and was just 100 feet wide.*
(Left) *Three massive explosions sent her to her grave.*

were crammed into every conceivable nook and cranny as the skipper navigated around the disaster area in the darkness of those early hours of Saturday morning.

The *Royal Oak* had been hit at a time when she was least prepared and with the majority of her crew turned in for what they believed would be another routine night. For the Germans it would be the first in a chain of victories that would give them a strong start to the war in which they wanted to reverse the defeat of World War 1.

As a tribute to the suffering of that night, a simple plaque was placed on the wall of St Magnus Cathedral, Kirkwall. The inhabitants of the capital were well aware that these lives were lost whilst providing protection for them. Out on the waters of Scapa Flow a green Admiralty wreck buoy marks the site of one of the most tragic and controversial losses in Britain's naval history.

The wreck of H.M.S. *Royal Oak* was immediately declared an official Navy war grave protected by law. It preserves the resting place of some of Britain's finest seamen who lost their lives in the worst possible way at a time of maximum impact for the German propaganda machine.

(Centre) *A green wreck buoy marks the war grave.* (Left) *Lucky survivors were picked up by the tiny tender* Daisy 2. *Had she not been there, nearly 400 more men would have died.* (Inset, centre) *The sign on the wreck buoy prohibits unauthorized diving.* (Inset, right) *A plaque in Kirkwall Cathedral has recently been enhanced by the addition of a bell from the* Royal Oak.

Scapa Flow

Located in the Orkney Islands, north of Scotland, Scapa Flow is a large area of naturally protected water whose facilities were considered ideal for the British Navy and her fleet.

Giving access to both the Atlantic and the North Sea, Scapa Flow is a good location from which to base strategic attacks whilst still providing shelter and security to anchored ships awaiting combat orders. Rarely over 50 metres (164 feet) deep, the Flow has an abundance of anchorages and only two main entrances. However, there are also five smaller channels but, prior to World War 2, these were thought to be impossible for a vessel to penetrate without being detected and sunk.

The collection of islands which comprise the Orkneys is best viewed from a light aircraft similar to those which provide the essential inter-island flight service for the inhabitants of the more remote outer islands. From the air you can take in the wide variation of scenery from the sheer 300 metre (980 foot) cliffs of Hoy, facing the uninterrupted power of the North Atlantic to the calm sheep pastures that flow down to the water's edge on the more sheltered east coast.

Approach from the south and you will fly from the northern shores of mainland Scotland towards the main entrance, Hoxa Sound. Hard to defend in times of war, this stretch of deep water would have been bridged with anti-submarine nets and constantly patrolled by armed ships. The tidal flow in this area is fast. One tide ebbs as the following tide starts to flow — given further turbulence by the waters of the Atlantic meeting the North Sea in the Pentland Firth. This stretch of water is notorious for its fierce currents caused by a gigantic volume of water trying to force its way through a narrow channel. This passage restricts the flow and causes the water to boil turbulently and swirl in powerful eddies as it waits to pass through from the Atlantic to the North Sea.

Continuing further north past the main entrance, you will see three much narrower channels which now have permanent stone barriers linking the islands which the channels separate.

(Top) The route of the German Commander's U-boat is now blocked permanently by solid stone barriers. In 1939, Kirk Sound was open, and the fierce tidal race together with old blockships were considered effective protection from enemy submarines.
(Below) The protected waters of Scapa Flow with Scapa Pier on the left. Royal Oak lies to the right, the oil seeping from her still clearly visible.

These barriers support roads that provide access from one small island to another. Convenient though they now must be, these barriers would never have come into being had it not been for the daring efforts of 30-year-old Gunther Prien, the Commander of U-Boat U-47. He had the nerve to consider it possible, and the skill to carry out an entrance into Scapa Flow through the narrow channel of Kirk Sound in pitch darkness and on a fast incoming tide.

This shallow channel is extremely narrow and protected by a fierce tidal flow. It was considered impossible to pass but old ships were positioned to restrict the width of the Sounds even further. Ironically enough, one of the blockships floundered on its way to Kirk Sound and sank before it could fulfill its final purpose. Despite its natural flaws, Scapa Flow is a sheltered anchorage that saw periods of intense activity during World War 1. Derelict buildings still remain as reminders of the active days when, at the end of World War 1, the German Imperial Fleet was interned in Scapa Flow following her surrender in 1918.

In a most surprising and bizarre

117

incident, the skeleton crews on board the German ships, rather than suffer the humiliation of surrender, opened up the seacocks and so, in one afternoon, sank their entire fleet. The scuttling happened so quickly and unexpectedly that only a few could be saved by beaching them. Most sank in deep water.

This incident has provided the Orkneys with a source of local employment ever since as salvage firms undertook to raise the wrecks and sell them for scrap metal. Most were raised in between the Wars but, for today's salvors, the remains of the Fleet have an added value in that the metal is free from nuclear contamination: they sank prior to man's nuclear activities. This added value helps to justify the heavy costs involved in raising the metal but few firms have made much money from their efforts. Nowadays, the wrecks are mostly left in peace for the diver to explore. They are unique underwater museums of World War 1.

With the onset of World War 2, the Orkneys and Scapa Flow once again became the focal point of British Naval strategy. The development of the aero-

plane meant that Scapa Flow was now more vulnerable to air attacks.

The Captain of *Royal Oak* was in charge of an ageing vessel whose orders were to act as anti-aircraft cover for Kirkwall, the capital of the Orkneys. Slow, compared to the more modern ships built between the wars, *Royal Oak* had just returned from exercises in the North Sea where she had received a battering from the harsh North Sea waves as she struggled to keep up with the Fleet. Her task of providing anti-aircraft cover was in response to fears that this war would be won or lost by the strength and effectiveness of either side's air attacks. To fulfill that task, the night of Friday, 13 October, she was lying half a mile south of Kirkwall. The night air was bitterly cold, the new moon was low in the sky and high tide was just before midnight. Everything was in Germany's favour.

H.M.S. Royal Oak

H.M.S. *Royal Oak* was built in the Naval dockyards at Devonport, Plymouth during World War 1. England, at war

(Far right) The first torpedo hit Royal Oak *in the bows. The second salvo was devastatingly effective.*
(Top, centre) Gunther Prien, Commander of U-47.
(Top, left) Metal from the German Fleet, scuttled in Scapa Flow at the end of World War 1, is valuable as it has never been contaminated by atomic radiation.
(Centre) Boom ships laid anti-submarine nets across the main entrance to Scapa Flow. They were opened to allow Navy ships into and out of the Flow.
(Right) Blockships are still in position today next to the Churchill Barriers which were built as a result of the Royal Oak *disaster.*

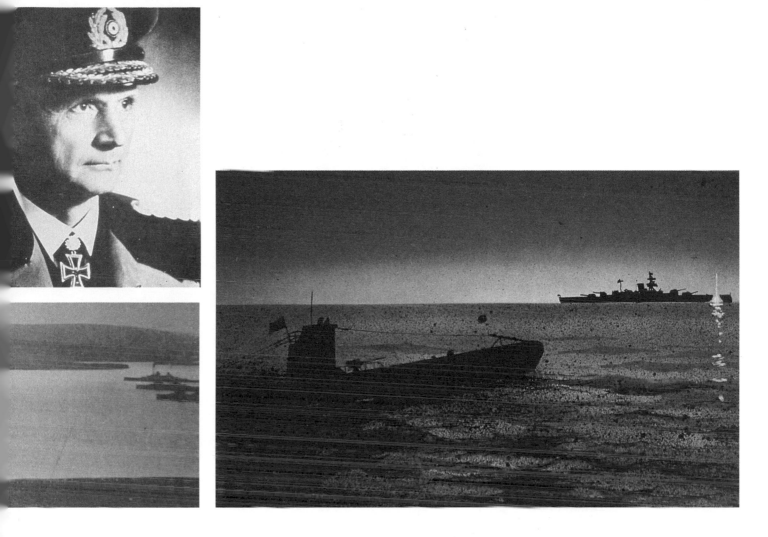

with Germany was urgently pushing forward with its naval shipbuilding policy in an era when battleships meant huge firepower and traditionally immense constructions whose very presence was enough to make any enemy think twice before engaging in combat.

Her keel was laid on 15 January 1914; she was launched on 17 November and completed six months later in May 1916. Nearly 600 feet in length and just over 100 feet wide, Royal Oak was equipped with a formidable array of firepower starting with 15-inch guns. They were the largest of their kind ever fitted to a British warship and there were eight in total in four turrets — two forward and two aft. Each barrel was capable of hurling their 900 kg (2,000 lb) shells to attack targets over 20 km (13 miles) away.

The scale of the machinery involved almost defies belief when compared to today's modern aluminium craft, fitted with computer controlled warheads capable of widespread destruction but fired from far smaller launchers. Supporting her main armament were 6-inch and 3-inch guns together with four submarine torpedo tubes although these were later removed as they took up too much space and needed too many men to operate them. Over 1,000 men were needed to keep Royal Oak at battle stations. She was a "Revenge" class battleship with four sister ships — H.M.S. Ramillies, Resolution, Revenge and Royal Sovereign. She served at Jutland in World War 1 and was capable of speeds in excess of 20 knots driven by her 40,000 horsepower oil-fuelled engines. It is this same oil that still seeps to the surface of Scapa Flow nearly 50 years later artificially calming the water and leaving an unmistakable patch, clearly visible from the air on a calm day.

On the night of Friday 13th, Prien approached Kirk Sound and, despite being half an hour later than planned, forced his way through Kirk Sound and into the calm waters of Scapa Flow. Once inside the Flow, Prien had to act quickly to capitalize on his chance of a surprise attack. His mind must have been racing as he surveyed the waters through the periscope of his U-Boat. His latest reports, based on aerial photographs, showed that several major British warships should have been at anchor in the Flow. Mercifully for the British Navy, all but the Royal Oak had set sail just a few days before to alternative anchorages, following fears that Scapa Flow was vulnerable to attack from the air. The Admirals were soon to discover that this misguided fear saved a tragedy from becoming a total and possibly terminal disaster.

With his crew at action stations and his torpedo tubes loaded, Prien fired a salvo towards the Royal Oak shortly before 1am. This first salvo scored a minor hit and helped to confuse the

C

crew on board *Royal Oak* as they could only assume that the muffled explosion was an internal problem which did not seem to be causing too much alarm. Their misplaced nonchalance gave Commander Prien the vital time to reload and within 20 minutes he was ready to fire the salvo which would score three direct hits and send H.M.S. *Royal Oak* to the bottom of Scapa Flow in just over 10 minutes.

The huge battleship listed heavily to starboard as the crippling explosions ripped open her sides and allowed thousands of gallons of saltwater to flood into her. This unnatural shift of balance was given fatal momentum as the main guns swivelled in their turrets and forced the ship even more off balance until she finally keeled over and sank.

Pulled down by the massive guns, *Royal Oak* would have turned turtle had it not been that the same guns and the flying bridge halted the rolling turn and brought the wallowing ship to rest. Her upturned deck lay upside down at a 45° angle, her sleek keel uppermost and her superstructure crushed on the seabed – 30 metres (98 feet) below the surface of Scapa Flow.

Today *Royal Oak* lies as she settled nearly 50 years ago. Initially, nets were placed over her to stop bodies floating to the surface. More recently the bronze propellers were removed by navy divers. Apart from these two interventions, she remains intact, resting in her silent grave. Her massive hull reaches up to within 5 metres (16 feet) of the surface at low tide and appears to be a natural cliff-face, so large is her area. The keel strip which runs most of the length of the ship, gives the first clue to a diver that this structure is definitely not an underwater cliff, rather one of the most unusual wrecks in the world.

The years have not been kind to *Royal Oak*. Her keel and hull, being in shallower water have attracted a thick growth of marine weeds and kelp which bloom in the summer months when the waters are comparatively warmer. Even this growth cannot disguise her overall shape in shallow water. The upturned curves of her hull slope down into deeper water to the main rails where the hull meets the deck. It is at this point that the whole atmosphere of the wreck changes and she takes on a much more sombre feel.

(Centre) An Airfix model shows how the wreck lies.

A   15-in gun breaches
B   Admiral's Barge
C   Torpedo holes
D   6-in side armament
E   Spotting top
F   Side rails

(Above) The Royal Oak's *upturned hull has covered most of her superstructure which lies crushed on the seabed.*

The upturned deck slopes away under the ship leaving a diver hovering in mid water with an 18 metre (59 foot) sheer uninterrupted drop to the seabed. Fortunately for divers, the gravitational pull of the earth is virtually eliminated underwater allowing you to glide down or rise up effortlessly.

Despite the confidence from near-weightlessness underwater, on the main rails of the *Royal Oak*, you have much more than physical emotions to control. Even the most experienced wreck diver will find it hard to equal the feeling of sheer excitement mingled with understandable fear as he leaves the rails to descend into the blackness.

The waters are dark and cold on even the brightest summer's day and the water clarity is poor. Visibility rarely exceeds 8 metres (26 feet). Plankton and other floating marine life cloud the water, hinder light penetration and give an eerie green tinge to the water.

As you slowly glide down, all you can hear is the sound of your own exhaled bubbles and the reassuring hiss of your demand valve as it supplies you with vital air. The dark outline of the wreck starts to appear out of the gloom and gradually you can begin to recognize detail. Everything is covered with a very fine silt which rises up in clouds if disturbed by even the gentlest fin stroke. Be careful when approaching for fear of reducing the visibility even further.

Out of the gloom your eyes search for detail. Gradually, as they become accustomed to the low light level, there emerges an enormous shape. Initially, you will not know what you are looking at or on what part of the ship you are, so it is best to start at a known point such as the stern or the bows and then follow the ship logically.

To dive on *Royal Oak* you have to be able to think upside down in order to recognize the various sections but, for a start, you can turn upside down for a while to view the ship as she would normally have been. This aids identification of a new area but soon you will start to think upside down and become familiar with large areas.

To swim from one end of the ship to the other would take an experienced diver at least 20 minutes. This is perhaps the best way of trying to appre-

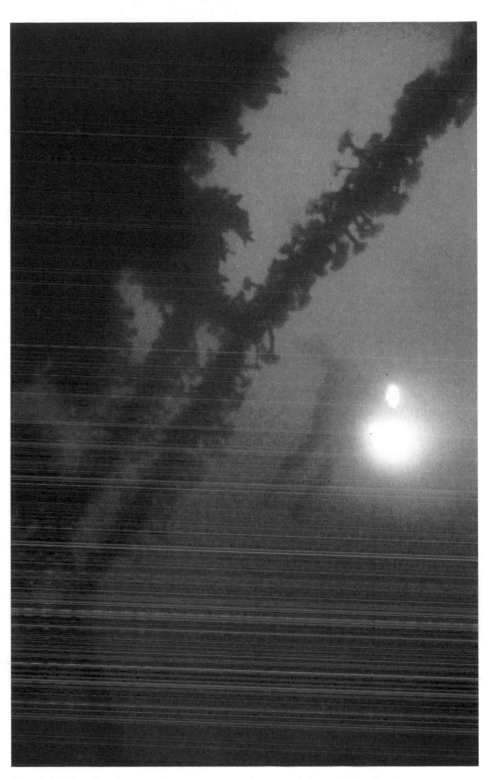

(Top, left) *The side rails now lie at a steep angle and point towards the seabed. Despite the cold, dark water, they have become the home for marine growth of all kinds.*

Most common are plumose anemonies. At this point there is a 15-metre (50-foot) drop to the seabed.
(Above) *The beam from a powerful underwater torch*

helps to light a diver's way and to show the marine life in its true colours.
(Left) *Loosened side rails dangle down towards deeper water festooned with plant life.*

ciate the enormity of this once proud battleship now lying crumpled yet intact on the seabed of Scapa Flow.

Having found the area where the deck meets the hull with the main rails, you can start at the stern and work your way forward. The depth is about 18 metres (59 feet) so your dive can last 60 minutes before you need to consider any decompression stops. As the waters are cold, you may well become chilled before the 60 minutes are up or you may run low on air and need to end the dive. Whatever happens, you have plenty of time to begin to view the wreck and form your first impressions.

With your ability to hover, you are ideally placed to view the wreck without disturbing her or the fine silt with which she is covered. Starting at the stern you will swim over the large rear deck area which leads up to the first of the turrets containing the big guns. With the deck upside down at 45°, the reversed weight of the guns and their turrets is trying to rip them from the decking. It is only a matter of time before the already perilously thin decking rots and will not be able to support the weight, originally designed to act in the completely opposite direction.

The eight 15-inch guns were in four pairs — two aft and two forward. As you swim from the stern and pass the first turret, you will immediately see the second turret with two more massive breaches, each over 2.5 metres (8 feet) in diameter. At this point the main superstructure begins. It is an area which has suffered a great deal of impact damage. Though the full impact and effect of this damage was reduced by the support of the main guns as they dug into the sand, there is evidence, nonetheless, of heavy crushing and disformation.

It is hard to express or even pretend to be able to estimate the colossal forces that are exerted when a vessel of such immense size and weight becomes unstable and surprised by a sudden ingress of solidly heavy seawater. For massive bulkheads to be bent and crushed with apparent ease, the forces involved must be huge. Areas have been crushed and twisted leaving hanging debris that presents extreme danger

to the diver. Always keep well clear of any overhangs. The reverse gravity, combined with the rotting effect of salt-water, have produced potentially lethal hazards. Despite the cushioning effect of water which dampens motion, the mass of a structure remains largely unaffected and any falling metalwork could prove fatal to an over-curious diver.

It is for this very sound reason and with a view to remaining alive that a dive on the Royal Oak becomes more of a visit than a detailed exploration. Only open areas can be safely inspected, leaving the dangerous areas and overhangs to be viewed from a sensible distance. However, this limit on your access does not impair your ability to gain an impression of the enormity of this structure. As you swim to the superstructure you realise the colossal scale of the ship. The Royal Oak must be the largest most intact wreck in such shallow water in the whole of the northern hemisphere.

Finning forward from the second turret and the beginning of the super-structure, the area begins to resemble a large scrapyard as the funnel and fighting-top lie crushed and pinned to the seabed. In her floating state, the fighting-top would have reached up over 30 metres (98 feet) above the main deck.

(Top left) *The main control wheel on the 15-in gun breach lies in 30 metres (100 feet).*
(Top right) *Outside the Imperial War Museum in London there are two identical 15-in guns to those on the* Royal Oak.
(Bottom left) *The breaches of the great guns on the wreck now lie in almost black water underneath the*

wreck. A diver's torch helps to show the detail.
(Above) *Detail of the 15-in gun breaches outside the Imperial War Museum. The main control wheel is at the top and a shell stands to the left.*

(Centre) *The section rear of the superstructure is a mangled heap of metal. There were no seaplanes on the Royal Oak at the time of her sinking but these are the remains of the launching mechanism. The seabed is littered with small debris.*

(Left inset) *The rear gun breaches are in much darker water than the forward ones. Here they lie right under the wreck in almost total darkness.*
(Right inset) *As the ship rolled over, the mast, flying bridge and spotting top buckled and came away from the ship. They now lie horizontally on the seabed.*

(Above) Water flooded in through these portholes and some survivors told of how they made a miraculous escape by getting out through them as the ship rolled over.

(Above, right) A 6-in side armament lies in 18 metres (59 feet). Most lie in line with the hull but this one seems poised for action.

(Below) The hull of the Royal Oak is lined with open portholes. They are over 50 cm (18 in) in diameter.

(Below, right and inset) The side armament plays host to marine growth which has taken nearly 50 years to form.

During the sinking, men in this area would have been helpless to escape as the structure quickly tilted over and drove into the sea as the ship rolled over. Only those who risked getting outside and jumping into the water stood any chance of survival. But they then had to contend with the ice cold, unforgiving northern waters. The choice was a hard one to make, and the time available to weigh up the options was fatally minimal.

In areas not crushed beyond recognition, you can discern the main gangways that provided covered access from one bulkhead door to another, with rows of portholes in between. Some portholes remain as open as they were that night whilst others are closed tight and even have their deadlights screwed down. The gaskets sealing the small area in between the deadlight and the glass of the porthole are still proving effective for there is air trapped in some of them — air from 1939 which sailors choked for and sadly found lacking as the chaos and panic of those 13 vital minutes passed by all too quickly.

Above these underwater gangways lie the side armament of 6-inch guns in single turrets. These guns are now above the gangway but when the *Royal Oak* was at anchor they would have been below and just above the extra protection bulges fitted to the sides of the ship to reduce the possible damage

from torpedoes. The bulges added a great deal of extra weight and affected the streamlining but the extra protection they afforded justified their inclusion. Unfortunately for the crew, if these

(Centre) *The ladder on the rear of the big gun cover now points upwards towards the deck.*
(Inset left) *A ladder in front of a 6-in gun gave access to the main deck.*
(Top) *The main gangway is now almost upside down, and the bulkhead door on the right remains closed.*
(Left) *A liferaft lies on the bottom. It might have saved more lives.*

side bulges had been twice the thickness, they may have withstood the attack.

Ladders lead from one gangway to another — up to some decks and down to others. They last resounded to the impact of heavy boots as panicking sailors desperately sought safety. Now these ladders attract silt and marine growth, their polished surfaces long since tarnished. Lights, with lightbulbs still intact, line the gangways but these would not have been lit on Friday 13 for fear of detection from the air. The safety of darkness suddenly became an added danger as the ship started to sink and sailors had to feel their way based on their memory of firedrills for just such an emergency.

Drop down towards the seabed now to view the scattering of small, unattached objects which must have fallen into the sea as the ship tilted. Of all these objects, none can be more poignant than the sight of a rigid liferaft lying upright on the seabed. Only some 4 metres (13 feet) long — she could still have saved the lives of many men had

she not been tossed into the sea or pulled down before they could embark.

At 30 metres (98 feet), a little further along the seabed, there is another small wreck. This is the Admiral's Barge, an ornate timber-hulled vessel tied alongside *Royal Oak* and used to transfer officers from the ship. She must have been pulled down with the Oak, and now lies upright and motionless on the seabed (see picture).

At this stage, the third of the four main turrets appears out of the green gloom. It has all but fallen away from the deck. The huge gun breaches are clearly visible on the seabed — the decking no longer able to hold their massive structures. Forward from here begins the large area of deck leading up to the bows. Here, the ratings would stand in neat formations at official ceremonies, proud in their crisp uniforms. Now this area, upside down, is a tangle of hanging ropes and a thick covering of marine growth. Vents that once supplied vital air to the decks below now are the homes of crabs and lobsters.

As you move along, the foredeck narrows until the bows appear, anchor chains stretching pathetically to the seabed. If you swim past the bows and look back, you can see the thin line of the bows which would have sliced through the water at speeds in excess of 20 knots. Drop down to the seabed again and you will see that the bows are in fact lifted off the seabed and light appears under the wreck. Only the foolish would swim under to explore. The sensible swim round and, if time permits, can begin to view the other side of the *Royal Oak*.

The other side is less revealing. As the *Royal Oak* lies at 45°, she is leaning on her starboard side. As a result, all there is to swim past on this side is a tall, near featureless structure reaching up from the seabed towards the surface. It resembles a vast, vertical cliff face, slightly softened by marine growth. You are faced with a 20-minute swim but with nothing to see en route.

Nothing that is, except for the first 30 metres (98 feet). It is in this area that the reason for the *Royal Oak's* rapid demise is revealed. It was in this forward area that the torpedoes struck.

The hull has been blown apart so extensively that you could swim into the hole and not be able to see either side until you stumbled on the inside of the ship. The metalwork is distorted beyond all recognition. Deck upon deck was flattened or reduced to mangled chaos. The area is in stark contrast to the other side where, even though there is extensive damage, the devasting explosions of the torpedoes did not reach. The twisted and mis-shaped metalwork that Prien's torpedoes achieved have not been disguised even by the camouflage of 50 years of marine growth.

Marine life

This north-east corner of Scapa Flow lacks the large tidal flow or water movement associated with the main entrance and small sounds. So the marine life that the wreck has attracted is plentiful but not profuse. Similarly, on the nearby World War 1 German Imperial Fleet, decades of underwater salvaging using hundreds of pounds of high explosives have discouraged fish. However, as salvaging work has receded so the fish have returned in both size and numbers.

(Right) *The inside of the gunnery spotting top is a mass of wires and machinery. On the night of her sinking, Royal Oak was looking for possible air attack, never imagining that a U-Boat could penetrate Scapa Flow.* (Top, right) *Marine growth now covers the once immaculate spotting top. This and saltwater corrosion are very slowly eroding this structure.* (Bottom, right) *The crumpled outriggers bear evidence of the forces involved when a ship of such size becomes unstable.*

Colourful wrasse inhabit the *Royal Oak's* kelp-covered keel, where ideal locations are to be found for their territories and nests. The abundance of nooks and crannies provides choice homes for all forms of crustacea such as edible crabs, velvet swimming crabs and small prawns.

In the deeper water, below 15 metres (49 feet), almost all areas are densely populated with attractive plumose anemones, some of which can reach up to 40 cm (16 inches) high with solid stems. Their base colours vary from orange to red and pure white, and their white polyps constantly stretch out in search of microscopic food floating past. Spider crabs scurry along the bottom as you swim past as if fearing you may suddenly swoop down and pick them up and abduct them.

If you could view the inside of the wreck in safety you would be sure to come across large conger eels who have grown fat in the safety of the structure. The labyrinth of passageways and tunnels provide ideal lairs for these long eels with the glazed unfeeling eyes, powerful jaws and muscular bodies, capable of propelling them far faster than any diver could swim.

These same lairs are shared with lobsters, whose night time feeding forays extend to the seabed. Armed with two large claws, one for cutting and the other for crushing their prey, these lobsters can reach up to 1 metre (3 feet) in length.

(Centre) The main torpedo hole is a large area surrounded by jagged metal. At one point a diver cannot see from one side of it to the other. Millions of gallons flooded in and the ship sank within minutes.
(Top, inset) Small anemonies now grow where once a sailor polished daily.
(Bottom, inset) Hauntingly named, Dead Men's Fingers grow on the wreck. Here their polyps are retracted.

Remembrance

Such are the living wonders of these
waters. But a swim along the *Royal Oak*
leaves an unforgettable memory of the
dead, not the living. This huge battleship, lying contorted on the seabed, is a
representative of a bygone era when the
importance of a nation was indicated by
the size and capability of her navy.

For the relatives of those men who
lost their lives on H.M.S. *Royal Oak,* this
wreck is a hallowed place. It is the grave
of over 800 men who lost their lives in
defence of Britain and as such is a
sacred and protected site. The *Royal Oak*
will remain on the seabed, protected by
Navy law and visited once a year by
Navy divers who, after a short service
conducted on the local coastguard
launch, dive down to the stern and cer-
emoniously unfold a battle ensign. On
land, survivors meet annually in Ports-
mouth, their numbers dwindle as the
years increase, but their short remembrance service keeps alive the love and
respect for both the ship and her ill-
fated crew.

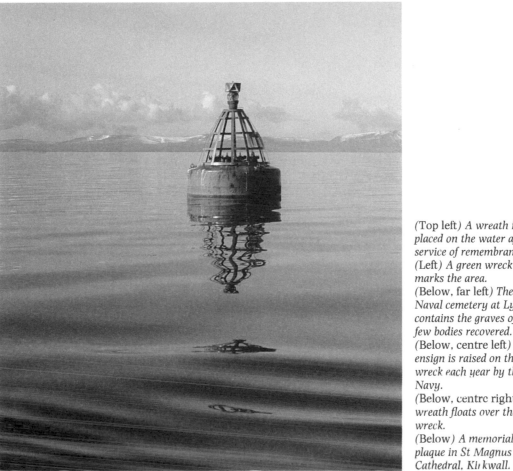

(Top left) *A wreath is placed on the water after a service of remembrance.*
(Left) *A green wreck buoy marks the area.*
(Below, far left) *The Naval cemetery at Lyness contains the graves of the few bodies recovered.*
(Below, centre left) *An ensign is raised on the wreck each year by the Navy.*
(Below, centre right) *The wreath floats over the wreck.*
(Below) *A memorial plaque in St Magnus Cathedral, Kirkwall.*

H.M.S. *Royal Oak* is a designated war grave, and diving on her is strictly forbidden by law. Peter Rowlands was granted special permission to dive with the Royal Navy in order to document the wreck on film.

THE
CRISTOBOL COLON

The Island of Bermuda has for centuries provided a stop off point for ships crossing the Atlantic. Her shallow coral reefs have also become the graveyard for many of them. Over the years, a great variety of coral has gradually colonized the wrecks, decorating them, and eventually engulfing them altogether. The three sections of the wreck of the *Cristobol Colon* make up one of the most beautiful wreck sites in the world.

Beneath the surface of the waters that cover two-thirds of our planet's extent lie natural marvels that rival any land formation for beauty and spectacle. Modern mapping techniques enable us to reproduce accurate models of the undersea terrain as dramatic as any in the Grand Canyon or Yellowstone National Park. Recent discoveries include huge submarine trenches and sheer vertical walls on a scale unequalled on land.

Of course, those pioneers who took to the sea centuries ago understood and appreciated the basic detail of underwater terrain — without the aid of sophisticated modern techniques. They were well aware of hidden pinnacles that rise steeply from the depths to form hazardous obstacles. Their navigational and sailing skills were often keenly tested in the shallow water fringing the reefs of tropical islands.

And, yet despite Man's achievements in mapping the oceans to make them a safer place, ships still go aground. Early sailing ships, with their billowing sails and multi-mast designs, had the excuse of being completely at the mercy of the wind and waves. The wrong combination of wind and tide could overpower even the most knowledgeable skipper and leave his vessel to flounder on shallow reefs. The situation was doubly dangerous at night: the lack of navigation lights meant a crew could only listen for the breakers to judge how near they were to land.

Modern ships, with powerful engine rooms, radars and bridges full of the latest electronic satellite-fed navigational equipment, have no such excuses — yet they still go aground and sink. It seems that human error cannot be eliminated, however much is spent on instruments and controls.

Perhaps one of the world's most feared ocean areas is off the island of Bermuda in the Atlantic. A broad expanse of shallow water reefs has brought disaster to more than 350 ships over the years. It is not by chance that the Spanish, having lost several galleons, called her "The Isle of Devils". The island's natural ability to be both a maritime shelter and a graveyard must make it the undisputed capital of the wreck divers' world.

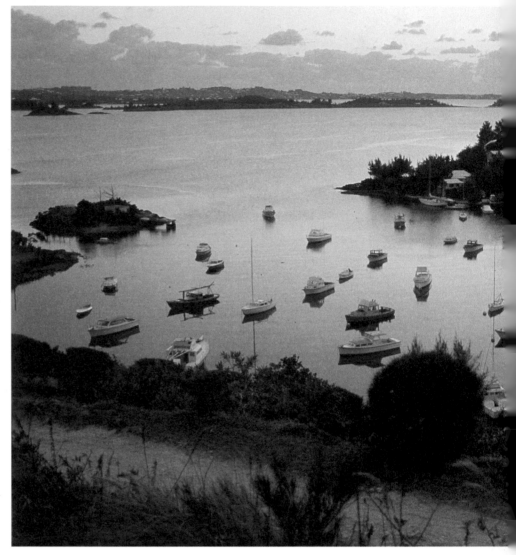

Bermuda

Completely alone in the middle of the North Atlantic, Bermuda, the world's most northerly coral outcrop, is over 950 kilometres (590 miles) from the nearest land. Volcanic action first thrust the island's land mass from the seabed, over 5 kilometres (3 miles) below to form an area no more than 33 kilometres (21 miles) long and 1.6 kilometres (1 mile) wide. For shipping, Bermuda is the main centre for the North Atlantic routes and this has brought trading prosperity to an island which has virtually no natural resources and is totally dependent on imports (the cost of which is supported by a financial tax-haven encouraging

multi-national company investors).

Yet for all her attractions to outsiders, Bermuda has striven to build a stable, controlled society and temper a tourist trade which, if allowed to take hold on this small island, could destroy the very nature of her attraction. An equable climate and superb scenery are enhanced by summer temperatures that are truly tropical. Winters are mild, warmed by winds blowing over the Gulf Stream which, at this stage in its journey across the Atlantic, is over 400 kilometres (250 miles) wide.

This mild and consistent climate has produced exotic flora and fauna on land with lush growths in frost-free soil. The lack of heavy industry leaves a sparklingly clean atmosphere with bright

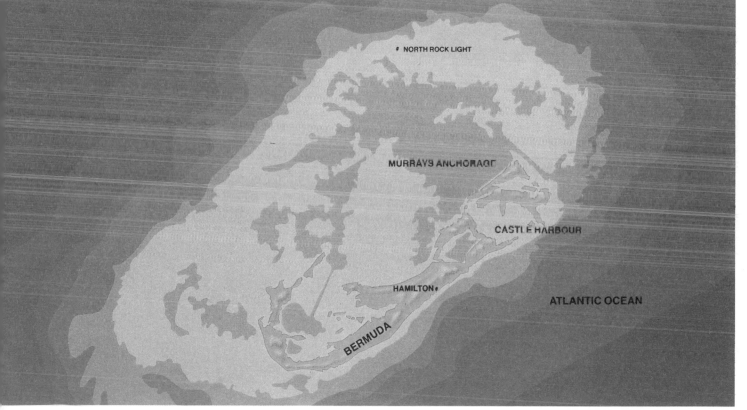

(Left) Bosses Cove provides a sheltered anchorage for small boats.

(Above) The pounding
waves have formed arches
rising out of the pure white
sand.
The lush Bermudan
climate supports (Above,
centre) Frangipanni,
(Plumeria Rubra),
(Above, right) Bottle
Brush tree, (Calistemon
Sp.), (Below, right)
Yellow Lily (Lilium Sp.)
and (Far right) Royal
Poinciana, (Delonix
Regia).

colours and naturally sandy beaches. A single airport limits the number of plane arrivals and Bermuda's laws do not allow visitors to come without accomodation booked in advance. Such controls keep Bermuda pleasantly uncrowded and encourage a society which derives the best from both British and American cultures. Bermuda has built up a reputation as being exclusive and therefore expensive – but for good reasons. To complement her land-based attractions, the Bermudan marine life is special enough to be considered unique. As well as supplying warm winds during the winter, the Gulf Stream provides a consistent supply of comparatively warm water. Even in the coldest winter, the water temperature does not drop below 15°C (59°F) between January and March while the summer sun warms the shallow waters to 29°C (84° F) between July and September. This consistency provides a comfortable marine climate in which the underwater life thrives. Creatures have no need to migrate to warmer waters during the winter but can remain in their habitats the whole year round.

For divers, the consistent temperature means comfortable diving for 12 months of the year. The clarity of the northern waters rarely falls below 20 metres (66 feet), and good calm conditions can increase this to at least 50 metres (164 feet). Despite these ideal conditions, the waters are not infested with boat loads of divers. Bermuda is surrounded by a shallow water fringing reef that covers nearly 500 square kilometres (193 square miles). In this sheltered area, the marine life is undisturbed and allowed to flourish in "greenhouse conditions".

Corals require clean, shallow, sheltered water to multiply and Bermuda has this in abundance. This naturally expanding location is the home of fast growing and rock solid corals which create natural structures of immense size and complexity. It is these structures that have caused so many ships to come to grief in the crystal clear waters surrounding Bermuda.

Bermuda – The wrecks

With such a history and supply of shipwrecks, Bermuda has a local diving population that spends most of its underwater time in search of and exploring the hundreds of wrecks around the coastline. The attraction is such that some divers have actually migrated to Bermuda for the diving alone. Almost all sites must be approached by boat – preferably of a shallow draft design to reduce the risk of damage on the coral heads. At low tide, proceed cautiously, with a look-out seated as high as possible to warn the skipper of approaching obstacles.

Boat journeys to wrecksites vary from 10 to 90 minutes depending on the site of your choice. The waters to the north where most of the known wrecks are situated are usually calm and clear. But judging distances offshore in the absence of any suitable landmarks can make exact location a time-consuming and sometimes fruitless exercise. There are times when the only way to find a wreck is to jump into the water with a mask and snorkel and be towed along by the boat!

In the Bermudan divers' catalogue there are about a dozen wrecks whose reputation distinguish them from the rest. They receive regular visits from the

(Right) *The wave action has opened up the wreck of the* Montana *for easy exploration.*
(Far right) *The bow section of the* Montana *is open and safe enough to enter.*
(Inset) *A diver examines glass ampoules on the* Constellation.

local dive clubs and dive tour operators.

The *Sea Venture*, which sank in 1609, can claim to be the very first shipwreck on the island. It was the survivors of this tragedy who went ashore to colonize the uninhabited island. As for the most recent wreck, it would be unwise to offer a name: new ones are added regularly.

The wreck with the most glamorous reputation is the *Constellation*. Most of her fame comes from her association with the film *The Deep*, from the novel by Peter Benchley, himself a keen scuba diver. The *Constellation* now lies six miles northwest of Bermuda but in 1943 was carrying medical provisions and general supplies to Venezuela. The cargo included several hundred bags of

(Left) *The huge paddle wheels on the* Montana *are breaking up but are still recognizable.*
(Below) *Two cannons from the* L'Hermenie *lie on the sandy seabed.*

(Above) *Soft corals
silhouetted against the
sunlit surface.*
(Top, far right) *An iron
propeller which will rotate
no longer, gripped by the
seabed and covered in
small marine growth.*

(Right) *The ribs of the
Caraquette lie upright in
the clear Bermudan
waters.*
(Above, left) *The bow of
the Iristo which sank in
1937. Her large winch
wheels are encrusted with
marine life.*

cement. These bags have long since split open and have concreted together to form a massive underwater pile and to serve as a useful underwater landmark to locate the wreck.

The variety of the rest of the *Constellation's* cargo makes it a divers' treasure-trove where interesting small items are still easily found. The most extraordinary part of the cargo was a collection of small ampoules containing a light brown liquid being shipped to laboratories for processing into painkilling morphine. It was these ampoules that gave Peter Benchley the idea for his book, *The Deep*, which was to be a follow up to his hugely successful first novel *Jaws*. In *The Deep*, the wreck containing the ampoules is discovered underneath another wreck found by two tourist divers (played in the film by Jacqueline Bisset and Nick Nolte). Peter Benchley did not, in fact, depart far from the truth, for this is almost what has happened to the *Constellation*. Just 50 metres (164 feet) away, 80 years before, the *Montana*, a paddle-wheel-driven ship struck the same coral head and sank. It is still visible today especially the 8 metre (26 feet) diameter paddle-wheel which now lies on its side in no more than 20 metres (66 feet) of water.

In a similar sequence of events, the H.M. Brig of War *Carnation* sank in 1810 on a reef near the *Constellation* and was followed 28 years later by *L'Hermenie*, a first class French Navy frigate whose 60 double-banked cannons were strewn over the seabed in just 8 metres (26 feet) of water. At least 25 are still clearly visible, together with piles of cannon balls and cannon supports. The rest have been gradually covered and disguised by the fast growing hard corals.

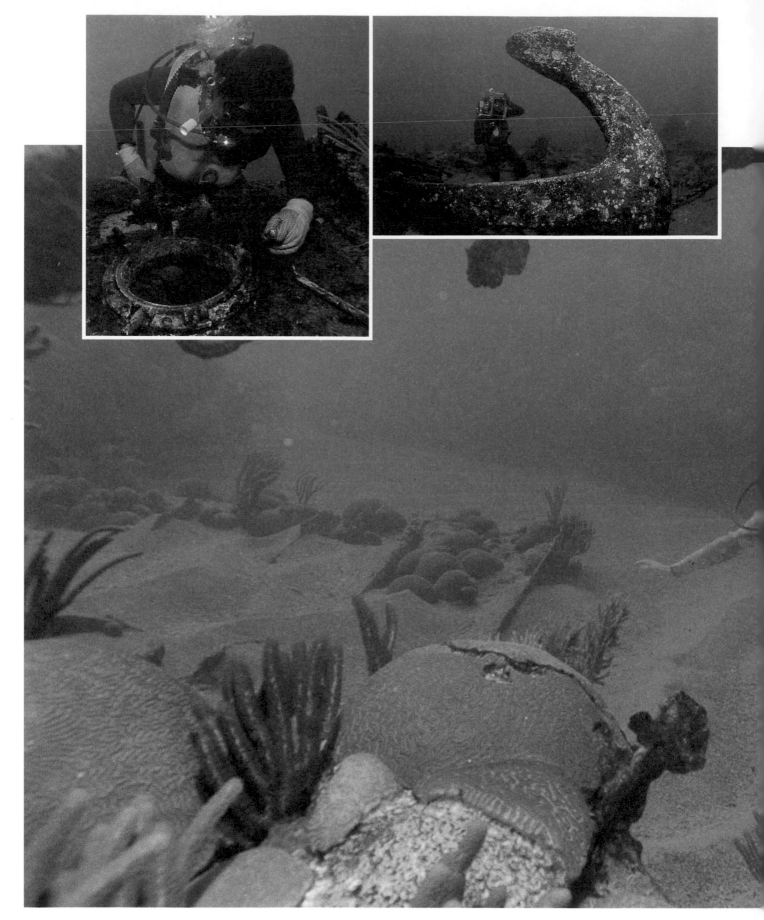

(Centre) *A diver framed in the wreckage of the* Madiana *which went down in 1903.*
(Far left) *Portholes are a prize for the* souvenir-hunting diver but they do not come off without a struggle.
(Left) *The elegant lines of the anchor of the* Caraquette *provide a* perfect "prop" for underwater photography.
(Right) *Marine life is quick to colonize and very soon disguises its host.*

In another incident, the *North Carolina* sank in 1880 but this time it was not the coral heads that were to cause the damage but the ship's own anchor which pierced her hull and sank her 8 kilometres (5 miles) offshore in 8 metres (26 feet) of water. Being southwest of the island the visibility is not as clear as the northern reefs but the *North Carolina* is an attractive site with an intact bowsprit.

The list goes on, well documented in local archives, and is being expanded each year as more wrecks are discovered. But, if one person could be singled out as the most successful wreck locator it would be a local man named Teddy Tucker. His maritime experiences include – to name but a few – wreck location, treasure hunting and shark catching for research. His reputation has spread worldwide and it was on him that Peter Benchley based the character Romer Treece, the boat skipper in *The Deep*, played so successfully in the film by Robert Shaw.

From such a rich harvest of shipwrecks, the one that is both the largest and most beautiful of all on the surrounding coral reefs is the *Cristobol Colon*.

The Cristobol Colon

Built in 1923, the *Cristobol Colon* was an impressive vessel, 480 feet long and displacing 10,833 tons. A three-decked passenger liner, she was built to cater for luxury-seeking clients and, in October 1936, set sail from Cardiff, Wales, heading for Vera Cruz in Mexico via Bermuda. She was under the indirect command of the Spanish Government, who had seized her during the summer to assist them during the Spanish Civil War.

The *Cristobol Colon* had taken on a cargo of coal in Cardiff but it was widely rumoured that she might be calling at Cuba to take on arms and munitions for the war effort. There were no fare-paying passengers on board so the crew of 160, which included six stewardesses, had a simple task during the voyage. It was the simplicity of this voyage which was to cause it to be her last.

At around midnight on 25 October 1936, a full moon was shining on the clear waters around Bermuda but the radio operator had his mind and ears tuned to a broadcast from Spain. Had he been listening more attentively to the much more relevant navigational signals, he would have been informed that the North Rock Light was out of order. As a result, the uninformed captain misjudged the channel lights leading towards Hamilton, the main port and capital, and the *Cristobol Colon* ran aground eight miles northeast of Bermuda. At the time, she was steaming ahead at her full speed of 15 knots and so ended up high and dry, with very little hope of refloating on the next high tide.

For two days after the grounding Captain Crescencia Navarro Delgado refused all offers of salvage. A New York firm was on standby with a quote of $1,800 a day plus $50,000 if they were successful. Even the local Admiralty joined in the negotiations but the captain was adamant. Local tugs tried

(Right) *The bows of the* Cristobol Colon *can be seen from the surface.* (Far right) *The propeller on the* Cristobol Colon *stands above the wreckage.*

to pull her off at successive high tides but it soon became obvious that the *Cristobol Colon* was destined to remain on the reef.

Standing so high and dry, she looked afloat from a distance and was a hazardous decoy for other shipping. Just under one year later, the Captain of the *Iristo* assumed that he was in safe waters following the *Cristobol Colon* but found himself and his Norwegian freighter aground on a nearby reef. To try to reduce this possible confusion, the masts and funnel were immediately removed from the *Cristobol Colon*.

For another five years, she sat on top of the reef, rusting and attracting a rich coral growth on her submerged hull. She seemed destined to crumble as the elements gradually took their toll but, in 1942, the American Air Force decided to use her as target practice for their pilots. They literally blew her off the edge of the reef and into deeper water. Her presence could no longer confuse approaching shipping and her structure began to take on a new role in the underwater world supplying a perfect sanctuary for corals and fish.

Diving the Cristobol Colon

Any journey over the coral reefs to the north of Bermuda is an extremely hazardous business. The area is so vast that it is impossible to stick to or remember a safe route. All you can do is to take things one at a time and keep a look out for local coral heads, whilst trying to steer a compass course in the direction of the wreck. Once on the outer edge of the fringing reef, marker buoys are often left to indicate the wrecksite as exact location so far offshore can be time consuming and sometimes totally unproductive.

Nearly 500 feet long, the *Cristobol Colon* was blown up and scattered over a very large area. Some estimates claim

155

between you and the sky. Light flurries of wind mark the surface with ever-changing patterns and give an enhanced three-dimensional feel to your dive.

So many wreck divers spend the whole of their time gazing down that they completely miss one of the most rewarding visual aspects of a wreck dive. The effect of sunlight on the dramatic structure of a wreck provides unlimited enjoyment for the eye and,

that her wreckage covers over 9,000 square metres (97,000 square feet) but there are at least three main sections — the bow, mid-section and the stern. Of these, the bow is in the shallowest water and a diver can enter at 5 metres (16 feet) and emerge at 15 metres (49 feet). Most of the finer detail has been eroded away over the years but deck railings still exist in this section. Here, passengers would have looked out to sea as they walked on deck after dining in the sumptuous ballroom. Large swaying seafans now replace ornamental flags as decoration with their roots firmly attached to the wreckage.

Most evident in this bow section are two very large propellers. This apparently odd position for items normally associated with the stern is explained by the fact that these two are spare propellors, one of which lies bolt upright. Each blade is 2 metres (6½ feet) high and these would have been bolted to the deck for safekeeping until needed. Being in such shallow water, the bows are gradually being covered by rapidly growing corals but it will take many years before these growths are sufficient enough to disguise this section of the wreck. Of all the sections, the bows are the most interesting and photogenic: you can swim in and out of large open areas. As a result you can access parts from below and look up to see the silvery surface that marks the frontier more especially, the underwater camera.

Most divers on the *Cristobol Colon* tend to spend a whole dive on each of the three main sections, and so have plenty of time to absorb the detail and scenery. In such shallow water, you can anchor over the wrecksite with two or three tanks of air and spend most of the day on the site. After all, it can take over 90 minutes to reach the wreck from the mainland so to do one rapid dive and return home would be a little extravagant.

With a fresh tank on your back and after a brief rest in the warm Bermudan sunshine, a short swim from the bow area brings you over the mid-section. You can see it clearly from the surface as it starts in 6 metres (20 feet) of water and drops down to 15 metres (49 feet).

(Above) *Delicate Sea Fans* (Gorgonia ventalina) *take many years to reach this size.*
(Left) *The solid metal sections of the* Cristobol Colon *will withstand the sea's erosion for decades to come.*
(Top, left) *The huge engines on the* Cristobol Colon.

On a good, clear day after settled
weather, you should be able to see right
down to the seabed. Two large boilers
lie with their tubes now corroded open
providing ideal lairs for moray eels and
small crabs. There were six altogether
that provided the steam for the four
1,775 h.p. turbine engines that were
running flat out when she went
aground. The area is littered with the
pipework associated with steam power
much of which was made from high
quality brass and copper.

Large numbers of valves and gauges emerge from the coral encrustation, easily identifiable since the glass fronts are too smooth to support the same marine growth. Still in evidence are two giant flywheels, both at least 2.5 metres (8 feet) in diameter, that once transmitted the power from the engines to the propellers. They are attached to the long propeller shafts which slope down into slightly deeper water. Although she was not damaged internally when she went aground, the subsequent damage inflicted by the American Air Force has reduced this part of the Cristobol Colon to a mangled and mainly flattened mass but, the cautious explorer can make out objects such as baths and toilets together with quality floor tiles.

The Cristobol Colon was designed and built as a first class passenger liner with plush carpets, mahogany-lined cabins and ornate light fittings. There was a chapel on board, complete with patterned floor tiles. In the mid-section area, lines of port holes make picturesque subjects for the photographer. Closer inspection reveals that they are just holes — the original brass fittings have been removed as souvenirs. Steeped in mild acid to remove the marine growth, they are then sandblasted before being polished back to the original gloss.

Ships that were designed and built as ornate vessels for the well-to-do are a wreck divers' dream. They always offer the chance of retrieving such small and fascinating pieces as finely inscribed

The powerful winches on the Cristobol Colon *play host to hard corals and divers.*

nameplates hidden under a pile of debris (the timber doors upon which they would originally have been attached having long since rotted away). On ships that carried wealthy passengers, a host of personal effects may remain to be discovered. But, unfortunately for divers on the *Cristobol Colon*, her last voyage was without well-heeled fare-paying passengers. Had that not been the case, her reputation would have been even further enhanced as a treasure-trove.

Lying slightly deeper in 15 metres (49 feet) is the stern section with some of its railings intact but, once again, target practice has reduced this once large section to a widespread area of flattened plates and buckled structures. Being deeper, a diver's time is limited in this area and there are still some

complete portholes, albeit in less accessible areas.

One drawback to this wreck from a tidy diver's point of view is the ship's main cargo: coal, that is now scattered all over the site. You may surface looking more like a coal miner than a diver if you are ferreting around under sections to try to find interesting and possibly valuable artefacts. Despite the warm water, most divers choose to wear a thin wet suit for physical protection rather than warmth. The wreckage can be very jagged and, with your view restricted by a mask, it is easy to snag or bump into it unintentionally, with the possibility of a nasty cut.

Being a civilian ship, the *Cristobol Colon* does not have any dangerous cargo, nor was she armed, despite being commandeered to help the Spanish in

(Far left) *The twisted wreckage of the* Cristobol Colon *frames a diver. The waters in summer are warm enough to dispense with a full wetsuit.*
(Left) *Large sections of the wreck are open and can be entered safely.*
(Below) *Huge nuts and bolts have been completely covered and will soon be unrecognizable.*

the Civil War. But, some of the airborne rockets and shells launched at her by the USAAF may survive undetonated and could be lying under the wreckage you are about to lift up. Salt water corrosion and seepage into the powerful detonation charges can make such ammunition more volatile. Caution is the best course: as a rule, never handle any munitions that look intact. Despite this slight risk, the *Cristobol Colon* has a good supply of brass shell cases which, when retrieved and polished, make excellent ornaments. In addition, when the shells are cleaned, intricate engraved markings reappear. Most relate to the year of manufacture but, on some, there will be details of flight patterns and of the type of explosives contained. It is the revelation of such detail long after the dive is over that makes wreck hunting so exciting and unpredictable.

The marine life

When you first enter the waters of a coral reef, your eyes will be greeted by a constantly moving colourful world of marine animals and plants. The corals that have set up home on the *Cristobol Colon's* structure include the evocatively named Brain, Tree and Staghorn varieties. All thrive in the shallows where light and clarity are excellent. Brain coral gets its name from its uncanny resemblance to the human brain once removed from the skull. But there the similarity ends. The underwater Brain is extremely hard and, although there are heads which closely resemble the size of a human brain, they mostly grow to over three metres (10 feet) in diameter. At such sizes they become perfect shelter for Gobies — small fish about the length of a matchstick with large eyes out of all proportion to their bodies.

The more flexible corals known as Sea Rods and Sea Fans are attached to a variety of foundations. Some mistake rope for a safe foundation and sway precariously in the current, their deep purple colour and intricate pattern of growth making them most attractive. As their name suggests, the Sea Fans are graceful, looking like intricately-

(Left) Elegantly shaped
hard corals thrive in the
warm shallow waters.
(Above) Detail from a
picture of Brain Coral
shows why it is so called.

patterned fans. The Sea Rods, more tree-like, could perhaps better be likened to giant cacti — without the spikes. Their colours vary between purple, brown, blue, black or yellow depending on their location on the reef.

Despite the wreck's position on Bermuda, the most northerly coral island, the marine life is typical of the region. But the *Cristobol Colon* has attracted some unusual inhabitants, such as the Yellow Coneys. These fish are a smaller version of the commonly found Coney (which resemble small Groupers). The Yellow Coney is quite rare and is a vivid golden colour. Aquarists who try to keep these fish at home are in for a disappointment. After about a month, the bright gold fades to a disappointing brown. As a saving grace, the flesh is succulent and tasty!

Most amusing are Trumpetfish. Very long and thin, they rely for survival upon a resemblance to thin strands of the Sea Rod corals. They hang vertically in their camouflage but are capable of fast acceleration out of the coral towards their unsuspecting prey. Being on the edge of the Bermuda Outer Reef, the *Cristobol Colon* often plays host to the open water species such as Barracuda with occasional visits from Tuna and Bonito. These fast swimming fish are large and valued for their texture.

It is not inconceivable that you could come across some small sharks, as you are over 9 kilometres (5½ miles) from the mainland and just 2 kilometres (1 mile) from the Atlantic Ocean floor. In particular you may see Nurse sharks

which spend most of their time on sandy bottoms. Their eyes are very small and fortunately their mouths and teeth are too. Despite being related to the more feared species of sharks, the Nurse is docile and easily scared off.

Perhaps the most exciting sight in summer months would be a large Manta Ray. These can reach up to 6 metres (20 feet) across but they too are harmless, feeding on plankton and staying close to the surface where they sometimes warm themselves on sunny days when the water is calm. For most of the time they keep on the move: you are more likely to see one swimming past the wreck on its way to find more plankton. They have been known to circle around and apparently pose for the cameras, and then depart for open water, simply and effortlessly transported by a flap of their huge wing span.

As with so many underwater sites where ships have come to grief and formed a new marine environment, you never can predict what you will see next. You are merely being allowed a brief visit into a constantly changing world. However, the sights and experiences revealed to you, on even the most mundane dive, will not cease to captivate you and drive you to the marine identification books to try and establish the name of your latest find. The beauty of shipwrecks is that they combine the best of diving with a view of human history. Add to this the unforgettable sight of the marvels of the marine life that make wrecks their kingdom and the picture is complete.

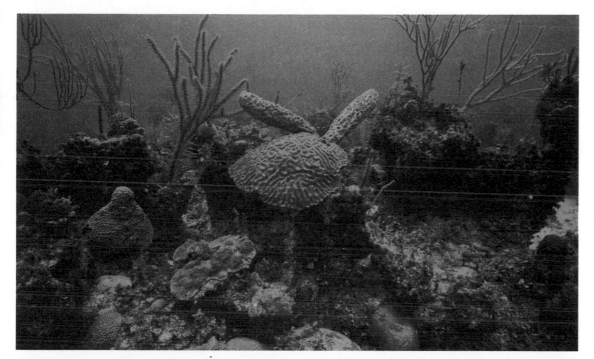

Bermudan marine life is both colourful and very varied.
(Far left, top) *Angelfish;*
(Far left, centre) *Porgy fish;*
(Far left, bottom) *Grouper.*
(Below) *Large clams are sensitive to light and movement.*
(Below, far left and left) *General scenes in shallow water illustrate the attractions of Bermuda's reefs.*

TRUK LAGOON

The events of World War 2 have left the
diving world with a host of shipwrecks to
discover and explore. The most extensive
collection lies in Truk Lagoon where
American planes took their revenge for
Pearl Harbour and sank most of Japan's
cargo ships. The Philippine Government
has protected the wrecks by law
preserving them as an underwater
museum.

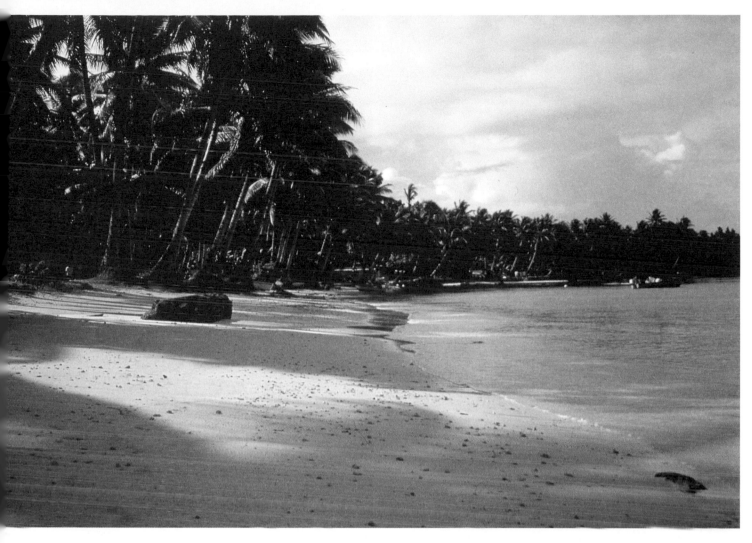

Once the debris and destruction of man's warring nature has been removed from the battle scarred land, a natural regeneration takes place. Although the result is environmentally pleasanter, the removal can destroy much of historical interest and deny us the chance of observing Nature's own regenerative powers.

In the same way, salvage of wrecks of naval battles, whether by governments for political reasons or by individuals for financial gain, takes place. Such removal denies divers the enjoyment of visiting the wrecks or their deep water locations. Occasionally, a governing body acts to save underwater wartime evidence *in situ*. When this happens wrecks can be preserved both for divers to view and for nature to change gradually.

Fortunately, many wrecks remain and become legendary dives in the subaqua world. Despite extensive salvage operations, the German Fleet, scuttled in Scapa Flow after World War 1, is one of the most accessible collection of warships in the world. There is, however, one location which can boast over 60 wrecks which have remained untouched for over 40 years. This is at Truk Lagoon in the northern Pacific. Here, successive governments have banned salvage and individual bounty hunting. The result is a unique underwater museum and laboratory. To divers, Truk is undeniably the seventh wonder of the world.

Truk is a natural lagoon about 64 kilometres (40 miles) across at its widest point and has a fringing reef over 161 kilometres (100 miles) long. This vast area contains 11 main islands and over 100 much smaller ones. For wreck divers, among its attractions is the evidence of a successful American attack on the Japanese Imperial Fleet in February 1944.

(Above) The beautiful tropical beaches of Truk Lagoon are sometimes scarred with the evidence of conflict.
(Top, middle) All wreckage is protected by law.

(Main) *Two Helldiver SB2c's fly over Guam during the Saipan Invasion in search of enemy shipping.*
(Inset) *Dublon Town, Truk Islands, was Japan's naval base in the Carolines. US carrier-based planes took this aerial shot just before the attack of 16 February 1944.*

As the Japanese Navy's main Pacific anchorage, Truk was under a constant threat of air attacks and its presence represented a hindrance to America's domination of the Pacific. On 16 February 1944, American forces began "Operation Hailstorm", an operation which at first took the Japanese forces by surprise. It was originally thought that most of the Japanese Fleet was at anchor there but, unknown to the Americans, just a few days before the attack, most of the capital ships had upped anchor and left the area.

In the attack, American Hellcat fighter planes swarmed over Truk's waters and inflicted a decisive blow to Japan's naval strength. They were followed by Avenger torpedo bombers, Helldiver dive bombers and finally the Douglas Dauntless bombers. The Japanese lost over 40 ships and 270 aircraft together with vital fuel depots. Further attacks the same year and in 1945 put paid to Truk's strategic importance. Once the war was over, the area returned to its former calm. The evidence of the American attack lay hidden below the lagoon water. It would still have been forgotten had there not been a plague of Crown of Thorns starfish in the early 1960s. To prevent these coral-eating starfish from destroying the reefs, the local inhabitants learned to dive. It was during this period of diving activity to stem the spread of the starfish that they discovered the wrecks and saw how nature had colonized them successfully.

World-wide, divers soon learned the attractions of Truk — wrecks, perfectly preserved, in warm clear water. Each successive dive revealed more and more wrecks. Over 100 wrecks have now been charted in and around the lagoon. Such is the number of wrecks that space is not available to describe them all in detail but there are two in particular which deserve to be singled out.

(Centre) The seaplane base on Dublon Island being attacked on 16 February 1944. Fragmentation clusters and incendiary bombs are being dropped.

(Left, top) A Japanese warship on fire after being attacked by fighter planes from the Carrier USS Intrepid.

(Left, below) Just off Dublon Island a Japanese ammunition ship explodes after a dive-bombing attack from a US plane.

(Below) A Japanese destroyer tried to escape from Truk, but was successfully caught by US planes.

(Bottom) The rich coral growths are the main diet of the Crown of Thorns starfish.

Fujikawa Maru

Lying upright in 34 metres (112 feet), the *Fujikawa Maru* at 435 feet long is one of Truk's best wreck dives. She was sunk by a single torpedo striking her starboard side just aft of the superstructure. Despite the fact that she sank in 34 metres (112 feet) of water, the tips of her two masts break the surface: they provide ideal mooring points for visiting dive boats. Over the years hundreds of divers have kitted up in the tropical heat, anticipating spectacular dives and, over the years, the *Fujikawa Maru* has never disappointed her visitors.

Diving off a large wreck in such clear water is ideal for most divers. The *Fujikawa Maru* is a wreck which can be enjoyed at all levels and by divers of all capabilities. The surface-dependant snorkeller can see the shallow water coral and can detect the shapes which lie in deeper water. Novice divers sensibly limiting themselves to 15 metres (49 feet) are able to inspect the main bridge, while the experienced wreck diver can spend each dive in a different area and still want to return for more.

As you hit the warm water and adjust your buoyancy prior to descending, you look down into the deep blue depth. There below you is a breathtaking sight. A blaze of soft corals grow on every available space on the two masts. Their colours vary from deep crimson red through to crisp yellows and light blues. Their polyps are all outstretched to capture the minute food particles which float past. Their stems reveal an intricate sub system of arteries resembling veins. They never fail to make an underwater photographer take just one more picture.

Descending down either of the two masts, you can see the main superstructure with the top of the bridge lying in no more than 13 metres (40 feet) of water. Since any sunlit area is inhabited by marine life, from a marine biologist's viewpoint, these artificial reefs are a productive area for study. Since the dates of the wrecks are known, the age of the growths of corals and molluscs can be accurately gauged. This makes the wreck a perfect base from which to establish growth rates and study the preferred habitats of these comparatively recent marine growths.

174

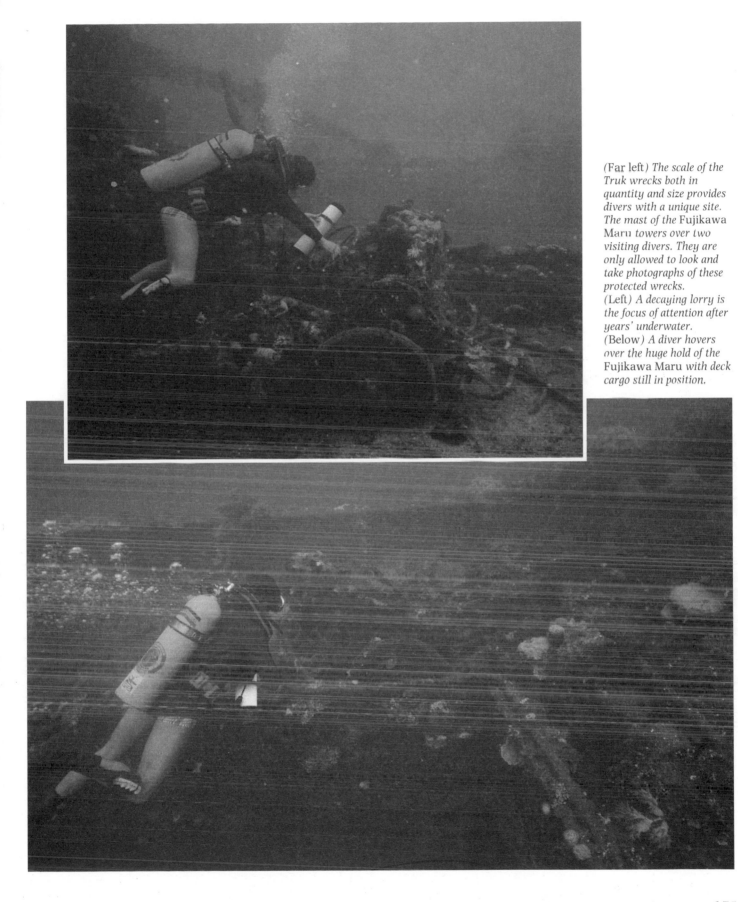

(Far left) *The scale of the Truk wrecks both in quantity and size provides divers with a unique site. The mast of the* Fujikawa Maru *towers over two visiting divers. They are only allowed to look and take photographs of these protected wrecks.*
(Left) *A decaying lorry is the focus of attention after years' underwater.*
(Below) *A diver hovers over the huge hold of the* Fujikawa Maru *with deck cargo still in position.*

(Below) The marine life has colonized every space on the wrecks. Both hard and soft corals compete with clams and colourful Butterfly fish come in search of food.
(Right) Intricate soft corals have delicate pastel colours and intricate patterns.
(Below, right) Hard corals cover the metalwork and soft corals add the final decorations.

As well as corals, fish have settled into the *Fujikawa Maru* as if it was always part of their underwater world. Large shoals of Glass Sweeper fish swirl around the wreck while Groupers guard their individual territories from unwanted predators. Moray eels take advantage of man-made lairs to house their long bodies, while beautiful Lion fish hide in the dark overhangs, waiting for night to signal their time to hunt and feed. Close inspection reveals an abundance of much smaller marine life but, for divers, it is the view of the larger areas of the wreck itself and its fascinating cargo that appeals the most.

The hub of any ship is the bridge. From this vantage point, the captain surveyed the scene and gave his orders.

This was the communication and control centre of the entire ship. On the *Fujikawa Maru*, marine silt now covers most parts of the bridge, but it cannot hide the details. Ship's telegraph, compasses, voice tubes and the main wheel, now interspersed with corals and the inevitable shoals of small fish, conjure up life as it once was on the bridge. Marine creatures make no distinction between the various pieces of navigational equipment. Their only criteria is that they should provide a stable platform for growth.

The *Fujikawa Maru* was intended to supply munitions and spares to support the war effort: in the holds, divers can see the massive amount of equipment needed to sustain a fighting force.

Of all the holds, perhaps the most popular is No. 2 where fighter aircraft lie on top of each other. In here the bright clear water allows us to see the cockpit of a Mitsubishi A6M Risen, commonly known as the Zero fighter plane. The instrument panel, complete with its radio dials and gauges, fills the space in front of the pilot's seat. The all important joystick is still there, giving the impression that the plane is ready to defend against all comers. Spare propellers lie scattered on the floor together with the various spare parts needed to maintain the planes.

Even though the ambient light levels are quite good, a torch is essential to see the colour and detail in the darker areas. The beam of a modern dive torch will penetrate great distances through clear water, but take care not to stir up the fine sediment which covers most areas. Once disturbed, it will take a long time to settle and it reduces the visibility instantly.

The light of your torch will reveal the true colours of the corals. Without the torch you would not see these colours, since water absorbs light and therefore colour. Reds disappear in shallow water and then oranges and yellows, until at 30 metres (98 feet) all you will have left

(Left) A fighter plane remains almost intact. Its windows have been shattered in the attack. (Above) The remains of a Zero fighter cockpit.

is blues and blacks. What looks like a dull grey coral at 15 metres (49 feet) could be transformed into a vivid red plant as your torch beam picks it out. Your torchlight will guide you while you examine the inside of the large wreck. The holds, large enough to swim in and out of, are safe to enter, but you should always be on the look out for hanging debris which when dislodged, is dangerous.

Examination of other holds reveals more about the *Fujikawa Maru's* varied cargo. Rows of 4-inch armour piercing shells together with row upon row of machine gun bullets litter the forward hold. Despite a thick layer of sediment over the whole area their neat stacking is still visible. Smaller less war-like stores include dozens of *sake* bottles and piles of pottery destined for the canteens on land and aboard warships. The glazed surfaces on the plates restricts marine growth so a quick wipe shows up the patterns as if they had been made yesterday. Some of this crockery would have been used in the ship's galley, still intact with its coal burning stove and array of cooking utensils.

Diving in and out of the wreck will almost certainly keep you at depths below 20 metres (66 feet) so you will have to keep one eye on your watch to make sure that you do not exceed your safe time. If you do, you will then have to decompress before surfacing so that gases absorbed at pressure are allowed to dissipate from your bloodstream without forming dangerous bubbles which would result in "the bends". The *Fujikawa Maru* is too large to be taken in on a single dive so most dive tours will cater for a second afternoon dive. A lunchtime break is an ideal opportunity to discuss your finds and learn from the experiences of other divers so that when you next dive, you will have a more productive time. The break is also ideal for an inevitable snooze in the midday heat after a light lunch!

To the north of the area lies Dublon Island and to the south is Uman. The waters around these two islands contain many of the wrecks but these are mostly lying in up to 60 metres (197 feet) of water. The safe maximum depth for air diving is 50 metres (164 feet) or less but, in the warm clear

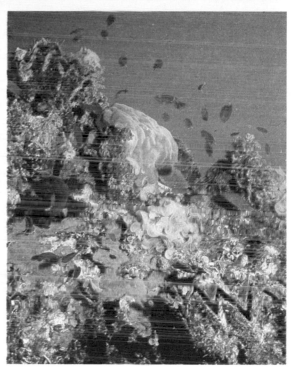

(Top, left) *The light of the flashgun restores the natural colours of the corals in these pictures.* (Top, top left) *The vivid colours of the marine growth have replaced the original paintwork.*

(Centre) *Marine growth cannot cope with smooth pottery surfaces so it is immediately recognizable.* (Above) *Small fish dart over the wrecks in search of food and shelter.*

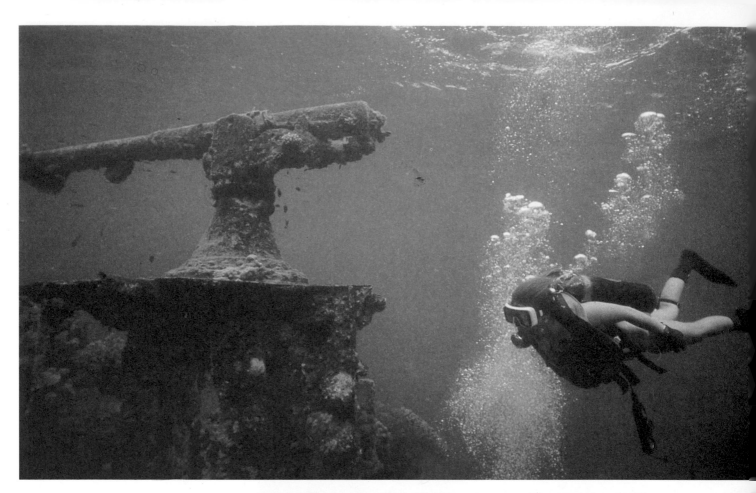

waters of Truk, many dives are made below this without incident. The wrecks are a magnetic attraction and justify the extra preparation needed for such deep dives. Being in comparatively shallow water, the *Fujikawa Maru* is probably the most dived Truk wreck both in terms of the number of divers and the time spent diving on her.

On a second dive you can go into areas missed on the first dive or not

(Above) *A small gun fitted to a cargo vessel would have been helpless in the attack.*
(Right) *A diver takes aim on the underwater world. The only shooting done now is with underwater cameras.*
(Far right) *Large sponges filter the clear waters providing contrast to the mast looming in the background.*

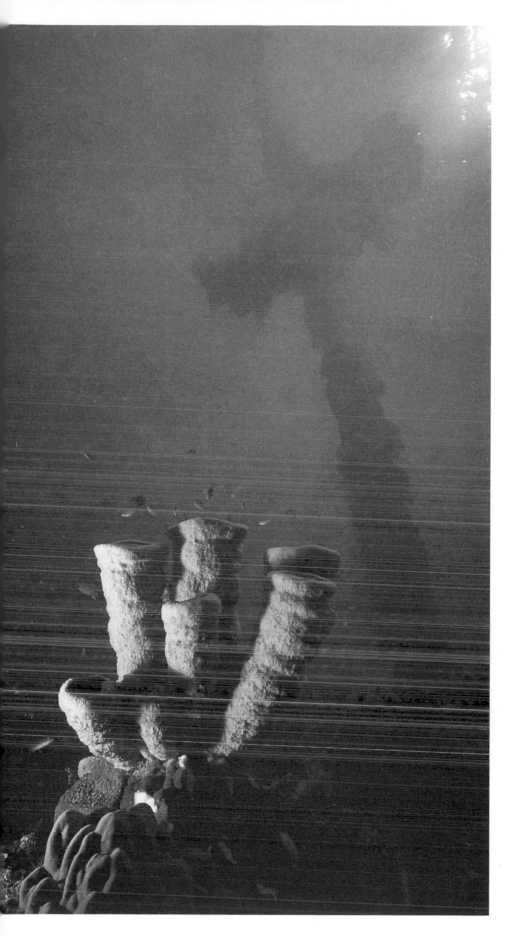

attempted during the morning's dive. With a little more experience of the layout you can swim to areas with much more confidence.

Whether you swim from the main superstructure to the bows or the stern you will arrive at a 6-inch gun. There is one at either end of the ship. These were fitted in 1940 when the Japanese Government commissioned her to be converted from a general cargo ship into an aircraft ferry armed with two 6-inch guns and an array of machine and anti-aircraft guns. The main guns date back to the Russo-Japanese war of 1899. They were certainly not the newest of guns then, but they would still have been capable of inflicting severe damage on any vessel which strayed within range.

Most divers want to have some sort of souvenir to remind them of their dives, and in this case, of a most memorable dive. Since it is forbidden to take anything off the wreck, underwater cameras are the ideal way of capturing the wreck without moving it. The host of corals make colourful foregrounds and the inclusion of a buddy diver will help to give an idea of the scale. Electronic flashguns help to restore the faded colours but, once again, take care not to stir up the sediment. This will be picked up by the flash and reduce the clarity and quality of the image.

It is almost impossible to know where to start when photographing such a photogenic wreck. The angles are limitless and the subjects abound. With only 36 frames in your camera you will soon run out of film. Particularly impressive are the two masts that reach up from the deeper water towards the sparkling surface.

A view up to the surface will show the sparkling sunlight dappling on the water and a deep blue circle known as Snell's window. This is caused by light being reflected from the surface. Shoals of fish are silhouetted against the bright surface as they swim in and out of their underwater habitat.

In Truk there are enough wrecks to last a wreck-diver's lifetime. The variety of wrecks is wide, their condition is preserved and there are new discoveries to be made on each.

Aikoku Maru

To the east of Dublon Island there is a concentration of wrecks which lie in much deeper water and so can only be dived by experienced visitors. The most amazing of these is the *Aikoku Maru* which sank in 73 metres (240 feet). She was 150 metres (492 feet) long and never had the chance to serve in civilian life. As soon as she was completed, she was commissioned to support the Japanese war effort and never fulfilled her original purpose as a freight-carrying passenger liner. Her forward holds were filled with munitions for her and other members of the Japanese fleet. In addition, she carried mines and other high explosives.

When an American Avenger torpedo bomber scored a direct hit on these stores, the resulting explosion disintegrated the whole of the forward section of this large vessel. The force of the explosion was such that one of the attacking planes was hit by the shock wave and it too disintegrated. The ship's fall to the seabed was instant as the debris of the explosion rained down over the site. Huge sections of metal were hurled 800 metres (2,600 feet) through the air and when the smoke cleared, the waters were thick with floating debris and fuel oil. The *Aikoku Maru* had literally been blown apart.

For those with sufficient deep diving experienced, the *Aikoku Maru* does not represent many difficulties as most of the interesting areas start at 40 metres (131 feet) but such a wreck needs time and close examination. Once inside her, you will discover a wealth of detail and tragic evidence of the human losses. You will soon be swimming down decks where the added depth will restrict dive times and so increase the time needed to decompress before surfacing.

This means that extra air is needed which is provided by using twin sets. The resulting increase in volume enables a diver to dive for longer and yet still have sufficient air to supply him while decompressing. Such a large supply of air in the hands of an inexperienced diver could result in a massive bend.

Suitably kitted up, the descent into the deep water is a time for adjusting buoyancy as the neoprene wetsuit com-

presses at depth and so reduces your buoyancy. Buoyancy compensators allow you to bypass small amounts from your main air supply into a life-jacket to give reassuring lift as you slowly fall down into the blue area where, as yet, you cannot see anything at all.

During such descents some divers experience a feeling of unease and disorientation. There are few indications of direction and the only obvious sign is from your bubbles which must be going upwards. As you fall deeper and deeper, the air being supplied by your demand valve changes not in taste, but in smoothness. The movements in the

valve are cushioned at these greater depths resulting in the provision of a rich smooth supply of air. This change is also amplified by the narcs. Like being tipsy, it is pleasant, but could lead to your becoming over-confident and therefore a danger to yourself and those with you.

The narcs has varying effects on divers and occurs at different depths but as a general rule a diver at 30 metres (98 feet) will probably start to feel some effect. Below this he will definitely be affected by the nitrogen increased air supply. The combination of the narcs and the *Aikoku Maru* itself test even the most experienced diver.

Just as the narcs start, the wreck appears out of the blue. The light levels have been getting gradually lower as the sunlight is absorbed. Your eyes become accustomed to picking out detail below and finally, the wreck appears. At first sight, the wreck is confusing for there seems to be something missing. She is smaller than you thought and this is puzzling. It is also disorientating, since you are trying to establish your location. It is then that you realise the cause of the confusion. The area forward of the main superstructure just doesn't exist. It was, of course, blown away in the attack. All that is left is an area of mangled metal, twisted out of all recognition.

Fortunately, the rear section is intact. Inspection reveals a passenger liner with attractive lines and a wealth of detail to explore. With one eye on your dive timer, you know there will never be enough time to see it all on one dive, so you must decide on an area and concentrate on it.

Swimming around the outside of the *Aikoku Maru* from the damaged bridge towards the stern, you will experience the eerie silence of the deep. This time the contrast seems even more extreme when you imagine the noise of the explosion which sank the ship. Now the only sign of that tremendous noise is in

(Left) The US attack on 16 February 1944 took the Japanese by surprise, and led to the end of Truk's strategic importance. (Right) Grumman Avengers flying in formation proved too much for the unprepared fleet.

the shattered wreckage. Your eardrums will register a slight pain as the pressure increases during descent and you have to "clear" your ears periodically to stop the pressure inside your sinuses building up to dangerous levels.

Anti-aircraft guns, which were almost certainly still firing as the ship sank, lie pointing to the sky. Rows of ammunition lie neatly stacked on one side and piles of exhausted shell cases are scattered on the other. The sun deck, originally intended as a relaxing area for the fare paying passengers, is now covered with thick marine growth. This is the most accessible area and is the starting point for an exhilarating dive of discovery.

At 50 metres (164 feet) the light is low and a dive torch is essential if you are to venture inside. Light can be seen through the ship which helps to keep down the rising claustrophobia which these locations inevitably encourage. Inside the ship, the electric cables, released from the bulkheads as their fixings rotted, dangle down and are a constant threat to the careless diver. As you navigate your way deeper into the wreck, the light disappears and you can only be guided by the light of your torch. You must know where you are heading. More importantly, you must be fully aware of your route for the return journey. That may sound simple on land, but underwater the rising bubbles from your demand valve crash against the ceiling and dislodge silt and debris which floats down and reduces the visibility straight away. Swimming forward is fine as you approach undisturbed water but as soon as you turn round you are faced with a completely different situation.

As if the ceiling debris were not dangerous enough, there is a layer of fine silt on the floor which can be over 30 cm (12 in) deep in places. Careless finning will raise this debris into a cloud which will take days to settle down.

The light of your torch concentrates your vision as you carefully navigate your way down passageways and through holds. The munitions in the rear holds which didn't explode, still pose a threat. Over the years saltwater can make them volatile so touching is forbidden, sensibly.

In the gloom, flick your torch from side to side to cover as large an area as possible to give you a chance to orientate yourself. On the *Aikoku Maru* your beam is just as likely to fall on human remains, marking the underwater grave of numerous Japanese sailors, as it is to fall on cargo. The skeletons and human remains throughout the ship are now made even more eerie by their covering of fine silt, as if smothered rather than drowned.

Personal effects can be recognized in the bunkbed dormitories. Metal picture frames, plates and glasses are easily discerned as they attract far less marine growth than items such as metal framed bunkbeds. The internal waters are still, protected from any currents, and the atmosphere is undeniably heavy. By now, we are deep inside the

ship and it is time to leave. Our visit must be well timed to make sure that enough air is left to decompress but the hardest journey is yet to come. The return journey through the silt disturbed passageways is not pleasant.

Your experience now is tested to the limit. Even the most competent can question the correct route, and any change from the proper course is potentially fatal. Ropes and guidelines, which must be taut, are there to point the way, but any slack rope is a serious hazard that can entangle and trap.

Nearly always there is the sickening feeling that the return journey seems to be taking far longer than you expected. The thought that you may have made a directional error looms larger by the second. With these feelings mounting up, the sight of the external deep blue

water again is almost like a breath of fresh air. For you know that you are safe by comparison, even though you are still 50 metres (164 feet) below the surface of Truk Lagoon.

The remainder of the dive is workmanlike and functional. Your dive timer tells you how long you have been down and you will have precalculated your decompression time so you know when and how long you will need to surface. As you slowly rise to shallower water you will be aware of the dark shape of the *Aikoku Maru* disappearing into the blue depths. Decompressing gives you valuable time for reflection on a dive which has been a series of contrasts – depth, destruction and the discovery of one more of Truk's wrecks that will continue to lie here protected in its unique atmosphere.

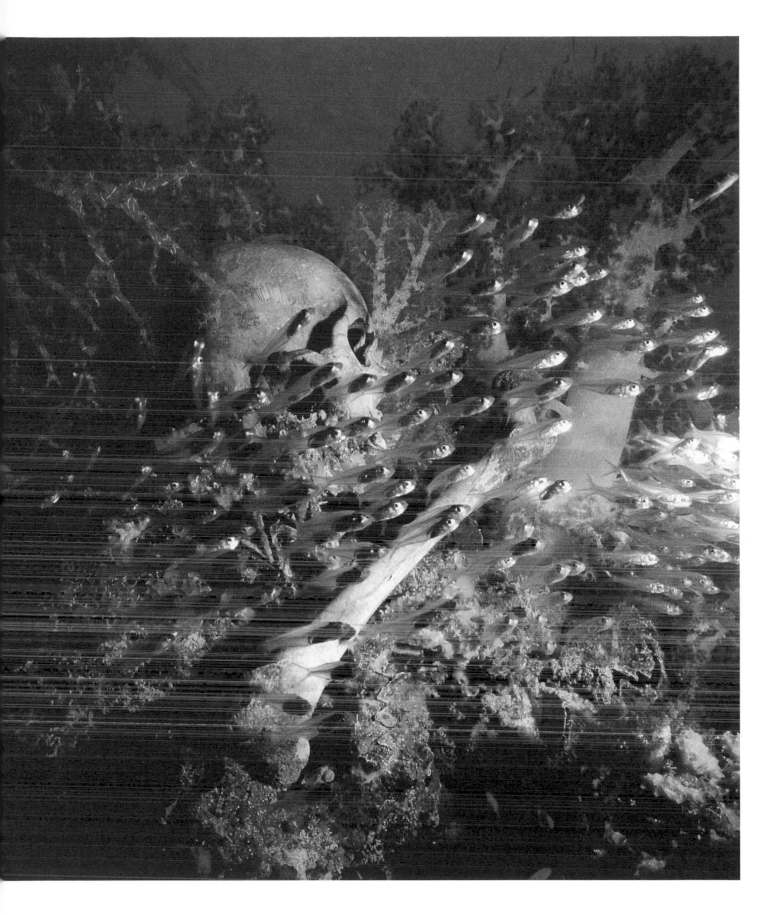

GLOSSARY

Airlift
A suction device that uses compressed air from the surface to dredge up soft material from the seabed for examination at the surface.

Aqualung
A device to enable divers to breathe underwater. Invented in the 1940s by Cousteau and Gagnan, it consists of a metal cylinder that stores compressed air and a valve or regulator with mouthpiece that delivers the air to the diver at the right pressure.

Bends
This is the name given to a condition that occurs if excessive nitrogen forms bubbles in the bloodsteam of a diver. Circulation is restricted and very severe cases can result in death or paralysis. Once the bubbles have formed the only way to remove them is by repressurizing the diver in a recompression chamber.

Buddy
A jargon term used to indicate a diving partner. It is always recommended that divers dive in pairs.

Decompression
After diving at depth for a long time it is necessary to control the rate of the ascent so that excess nitrogen can be released gradually from the bloodstream to prevent the formation of minute circulation-stopping bubbles. This is done by stopping at specific depths for a certain time before reaching the surface. The length of time is laid down in tables issued by all major diving authorities. Failure to adhere to these time limits could result in the BENDS.

Drysuit
This is an insulated, waterproof suit used for cold water diving. It has a waterproof zip and seals on the neck, wrists and ankles to prevent water entering the space around the body.

Marker buoy
A float with a line attached that the diver secures to an underwater "find" to make it simple to locate later.

Nitrogen Narcosis
A temporary euphoric effect caused by the pressure of nitrogen in the bloodsteam. It usually starts at a depth of around 30 metres (100ft). It is also known as "narcs" or "raptures of the deep".

Recompression chamber
This is a sealed compartment, usually cylindrical, into which divers are placed for recompression if they show any symptoms of the BENDS. It allows them to be pressurized as if they were underwater. The pressure is controlled from outside the chamber.

Slates
Rigid plastic sheets with waterproof markers attached, on which divers can write messages to each other underwater.

Tanks
Also known as cylinders or bottles, they contain compressed air and are attached to the diver's back by a harness.

Thermocline
This is the dividing point between layers of water of differing temperatures. There can be as many as three in divable depths.

Valve
Also known as a regulator, it is fitted to the compressed air cylinder and delivers air via the mouthpiece to the diver.

Weightbelt
A belt containing varying amounts of lead. It is used to adjust a diver's buoyancy underwater.

Wetsuit
Usually made from neoprene, it is a suit that traps a thin layer of water around the diver's body. The layer of water is heated by the body and insulated by the neoprene. It is widely used in all areas of diving, though in really warm waters it would probably only be worn as a form of protection.

INDEX

Page numbers in *italic* refer to the illustrations

ACKNOWLEDGEMENTS

T = top, B = bottom, C = centre, R = right, L = left

PHOTOGRAPHERS
Paul Arbiter 24BL, 25, 29T, 30C, 35.
Geoff Barker 63, 70–79.
BBC Hulton Picture Library 8R.
Steve Birchall 45TR, 120C, 121BR.
Mensun Bound 13, 18B, 19TL, 19TR, 19C, 19B, 21T, 21B, 22, 23, 24R, 26, 27, 28TR, 28BR, 28CL, 28BL, 29BL, 29BR, 30T, 31TR, 31C, 31B, 32CL, 34, 37T, 37BL, 37BR.
Canada House, London 64, 66–67.
Horace Dobbs 167, 174–177, 182T, 182B, 186–187, 188.
Alex Double 87B, 91, 94–95B, 100–101, 101BL, 102T, 103TL, 108CL.
Tamara Double 88–89.
Laurence Gould 141, 142–161.
Imperial War Museum 112–113.
Jack Jackson 82–83T, 86–87T, 86B, 92, 93B, 95T, 96TL, 99T, 99BR, 100CT, 100BR, 103BL, 104–105, 106TR, 106C, 107TL.
Bill Lewis/Bruce Bailey 168TR, 169T, 179, 180TL, 180TR, 180BR, 181T.
The Mansell Collection 7L, 9L.
Michael Holford Library 16BL, 17T, 17B.
Leo Mastogastino 36.
Keith Morris Title Page 1, Title Page 2, 18T,

56L, 58BL, 58–59, 59TR, 60–61, 81, 83B, 84–85, 93T, 96TR, 96CL, 98, 102B, 103BR, 106–107, 106BL, 107TR, 107CR, 107BR, 108 except CL, 109, 137B, 162–163, 164–165, 177TL.
National Archive Washington DC 170–171, 172–173(B/W), 184–185.
Oxford University World Ship Trust 14–15, 20TR, 31TL, 32T, 33.
Peter Rowlands End papers; 12–13, 38–39, 42B, 43, 44, 45B, 46TL, 46BL, 47, 48BL, 49, 50–51, 52T, 52B, 53, 54–55, 57T, 57BR, 62–63, 80–81, 90, 94TL, 96–97, 99BL, 110–111, 113TL, 114, 119, 120TL, 120TR, 120BL, 120CB, 120BR, 122–136, 137T, 138–141, 166–167, 173BR.
Peter Sieniewicz 69T, 69B.
Herwath Voigtman: Planet Earth Pictures: 178, 180–181B, 183, 189.
Adam Woolfitt: Susan Griggs Agency 6BL.
World's Edge Picture Library 7R, 8L, 8R.
ILLUSTRATIONS
Mensun Bound 20, 23, 26, 30–31, 34.
Caroline Caldwell 16. **John Charles** 15, 40–41, 65, 68, 82, 116, 143, 168.
Simon Dobbs 37. **Hugh Morrison** 36.
Francis Rankin 32. **Mike Wright** 33.